A D

YOUR POCKET

Nerys Dee

Thorsons

TO BILL

WHO MADE MY DREAMS COME TRUE

Thorsons
An Imprint of HarperCollins*Publishers*
77–85 Fulham Palace Road,
Hammersmith, London W6 8JB

The Thorsons website address is: www.thorsons.com

First published as *Your Dreams and What They Mean* 1984, 1995
This revised edition published 2001

1 3 5 7 9 10 8 6 4 2

© Estate of Nerys Dee 1984, 1991, 2001

Nerys Dee asserts the moral right
to be identified as the author of this work

A catalogue record for this book
is available from the British Library

ISBN 0 00 712352 3

Printed and bound in Great Britain by
Martins the Printers Ltd, Berwick-upon-Tweed

CONTENTS

INTRODUCTION

Dreams are as much a part of our lives as everything else we experience. Not only can they help us to understand ourselves, other people and those difficult situations in which we so often find ourselves, they show us glimpses of the future, solve our problems and help us heal ourselves, too.

We all dream, even those who insist that they never do. The difference between the dreamer and the supposed non-dreamer is that one remembers his dreams whereas the other does not. Since we sleep on average for one-third of each day it means that by the time we are 75 years old we have slept for 25 years, and for at least 10 of them we have been dreaming. This is a lot of dreaming, but we still do not really know what a dream is – nor, for that matter, what sleep is.

Generally we think of dreams as visual experiences, but what of non-visual dreams? We have five senses; sight is only one of these. Added to this we have what is often called a sixth sense, and this includes intuitiveness and psychic awareness.

To the ancients, dreams were messages from the gods, but today they are regarded as emotional expressions from our innermost selves. Since dreams reflect life in all its many aspects from the mundane to the mysterious, both the beliefs of the ancients and those of today are correct in their own way and from their different standpoints, for dreams are all things to all people.

As a dream analyst it is the dream I analyse, not the dreamer. To me dreams are highly personal messages from ourselves to ourselves, so obviously the best person to interpret and understand them is the dreamer who created them. This, however, does not mean that someone else cannot discover the messages hidden in another's dream, because they can. What they cannot do is to apply that message with its personal associations to the dreamer's own situation or circumstances. Only the dreamer can do this. As an example, the dream message that warns the dreamer of a person who owns, say, a blue car and has a tall tree in their garden means absolutely nothing to the interpreter, but to the dreamer, who alone recognizes this person, it may mean everything. When interpreting dreams for others it is, therefore, very important not to impose our own association of ideas, collected through our own experiences in life, onto their dream messages.

The interpretation of dreams is only one aspect of the whole concept of dreaming. Dreams are potential sources of great wisdom and guidance, and there is much we can do to delve into this enormous reservoir and so receive answers to problems, to order as it were. This is exactly what the ancients did thousands of years ago when they practised the art of dream incubation, so why not now? The incubation of dreams is simply a request made to ourselves, to God or to those universal forces once known as gods and goddesses. C. G. Jung called them archetypes. Dream incubation encompasses life, so having the right dream at the right time can help with practical, down-to-earth problems just as easily as it can bring flashes of enlightenment and inspiration from heavenly heights.

Practice makes perfect, so the more dreams we have the easier it becomes to understand them. With the help of a dictionary, the meanings of signs and symbols can be discovered, but no dictionary can do more than this. It cannot, for example, tell us whether a dream is literal, symbolic or a mixture of both. This is what we need to know first of all. Once an interest in dreams has been kindled, however, the rest is easy. Even if that interest is only fleeting, like some of our dreams, the important thing is that we carry on dreaming and at least recognize and respect our dreams for what they are.

Nerys Dee

CHAPTER ONE

OUR DREAMING PAST: DREAMS IN HISTORY AND ART

Egyptian, Babylonian, Middle Eastern, Hebrew, Celtic, Greek, Arabic, Indian, Chinese, Japanese, French and Russian cultures all possess ancient records showing the important part dreams played not only in the lives of individuals but in shaping the heritage and destiny of these people as a whole. Religions, philosophies, the classics, history, politics, science and the arts all owe far more to the subtle power of dreams than is generally realized.

Looking back over the centuries at certain dreams experienced by mankind, it is clear to see the effect these have had on history and on our way of life. Every type of dream possible has been experienced by the famous and the infamous, and whether inventive or creative, warning or prophetic, many have been woven into the colourful histories of every nation on earth.

One of the oldest recorded dreams is to be found in Mesopotamian literature, prophesying a gloomy impending disaster. The hero who dreamed this described a huge tidal wave engulfing and swamping much of the face of the earth; in detail very similar to the biblical account of the Flood.

Dreams and dream interpretations were forms of divination used extensively by ancient cultures all over the world. Like oracles generally, dreams were believed to express the will of the gods and their divine instructions. The seeking of dreams which would invoke the special powers of the gods is known as *incubation*, and although ways of doing this varied in detail, in principle they were much the same throughout the ancient world. Incubation is defined as sleeping in a sanctuary with the intention of receiving a dream-reply to a question asked of a god or goddess, having first performed certain rituals. Greek and Latin literature is full of examples of this form of communication with the gods.

The oldest dream book in the world is thought to be a collection of Assyrian, Babylonian and Egyptian dream-lore collectively called Artimedorous's Oneiro-Critica.

Classical philosophers tried hard to explain the mysteries of sleep and dreams in terms of physical causes. Plato, for example, thought that the liver was the seat of dreams. Galen saw all dreams as health warnings, as did Cicero, but Aristotle believed them to be a mental effect from a physical cause. Democritus, on the other hand, considered them to be brought about by 'things floating in the atmosphere which attacked the spirit during sleep'. Pliny believed them to be entirely supernatural in origin, but it was Hippocrates, the father of medicine, who probably came nearest to the truth when he said, 'Some dreams are divinely inspired but others are the direct result of the physical body.'

Although Greek philosophers of the day studied the cause of dreams, members of the public were more interested in their meanings, for to them they were very important sources of information. Dream interpreters were therefore in great demand and consulted in much the same way as doctors are today. The difference was that these 'doctors' were expected to discover, from dreams, solutions to personal problems as well as remedies for the body.

THE GATE OF DREAMS

Most dreams, however, were seen as either warnings or prophecies. A warning dream meant that trouble could be avoided if its message was acted upon, but nothing could be done about a situation if it was prophetic. To decide which of these a dream was, a method known as the Gates of Dreams was used. There were, apparently, two dream gates, one of ivory and one of horn. If a dream passed through the Ivory Gate it was a warning, but if it passed through the Horn Gate it was prophetic. Our dreaming minds love puns, so it is not surprising that these symbolic gates were created from such a play on words. The Greek for ivory is 'elephas', also meaning to cheat, and the Greek for horn is 'karanoo', also meaning to accomplish. Together, they represent that which can be averted and the inevitable!

One of the richest sources of dreams from the ancient world comes from the Bible. In the Old and New Testaments there are over 20 well-documented accounts of dreams, each offering in different ways divine guidance in the form of warnings and prophecies. These messages were so powerful that in retrospect it can be seen how, by acting upon the advice given, the dreamers actually steered the destiny of nations, and so, in many instances, altered the course of history.

Dreams in the Bible fall into two distinct types: literal and symbolic. In one, God or His messenger speaks directly to the dreamer and gives him explicit instructions which need little or no interpretation. In the other, the messages are symbolic, appearing in the form of parables. These need considerable thought and interpretation before their meanings can be extracted. As biblical interpreters, it is Joseph and Daniel who emerge as the experts, but all Hebrews were well versed in this art and had little trouble recognizing the messages contained in their dreams.

It is expressly stated in the Bible that God speaks to man in his dreams: 'For God speaketh once, yea twice, yet man perceiveth it not. In a dream, in a vision of the night when deep sleep falleth upon men slumbering upon their bed, then He openeth their ears and sealeth in their instructions.' (Job 33:14–16). The first dream in the Old Testament is an excellent example of this direct communication with its literal meaning abundantly clear! 'God came to Abimelech in a dream by night and said to him "Behold! thou art but a dead man for the woman thou hast taken is another man's wife." ' (Genesis 20:3).

Jacob's famous dream involving the ladder which stretched down from heaven above to the earth below was both literal and symbolic, as the following extract shows: 'And he dreamed and behold a ladder set up on the earth and the top of it reached to heaven: and behold the angels of God were ascending and descending on it. And behold! The Lord stood above it and said "I am the Lord God of Abraham the father and the God of Isaac; the land whereon thou liest, to thee will I give, and to thy seed." ' (Genesis 28:12). In a later dream just after departing from Labon, Jacob again receives God's instructions but this time via an angel. 'And the angel of God spoke unto me in a dream saying "Jacob", and I said, "Here I am." And he said, "Lift up thine eyes and see, all the rams which leap upon the cattle are ringstraked, speckled and grisled. Now arise and return unto thy land of thy kindred."' (Genesis 31:11–13). Acting as an intermediary, the angel's role in this dream is similar to that of Zeus's messengers, the underworld helpers of An-Za-Oar, the god of the Sumerians, Babylonians and the Assyrians and, in fact, bringers of dreams throughout the ancient world.

Moses, we are told, was instructed by God to listen for His words in his dreams: 'Hear now my words. If there be a prophet among you, I the Lord will make myself known to him in a vision and will speak to him in a dream.'

The early Christian fathers regarded dreams in much the same way as did the prophets of the Old Testament. Gregory of Nyssar in the 4th century AD accepted them as divine messages and even believed them to be mirrors of the soul which reflected the personality of the dreamer. In his work entitled *On Making Man* he wrote that from these visions it was possible to better understand and value one's true self. St Augustine used his dreams as channels of communication between himself, God and His angels, and he repeatedly requested them to maintain his 'chaste desires'. Thomas Aquinas, a seer in the Old Testament sense, wrote extensively about the prophetic nature of dreams and suggested 'a single cause of both the dream and the event', a concept later to be echoed by Carl Jung.

DREAM ORACLES IN JAPAN

There are many accounts of dream oracles throughout medieval Japanese literature, and from these we learn that there were places of incubation in both Shinto and Buddhist temples. One celebrated Shinto shrine at Usa in Kyushi was dedicated to the god Hachiman. Among the Buddhist temples three in particular were famous as dream oracles and dedicated to the Bodhisattva Kannon.

Sickness was prominent among the troubles which impelled people to seek help from their dreams. A 15th-century collection of stories known as Hasedra Reigenki describes the healing miracles achieved from dream communication with the gods. One of these tells of a man who, disfigured by leprosy, journeyed to Hasedra and after seven days and seven nights in seclusion dreamed that a boy appeared from the inner sanctum and said, 'Your sickness is very difficult to cure because it is due to karma from a past life. But Kannon has nevertheless commanded me to heal you.' The boy then licked the man all over and when he awoke in the morning he found himself clean and cured.

Problems other than health were solved by dream oracles, too. An inscription shows how a priest, unable to remember a very difficult passage by heart, learned it in one night of dreaming. And a man, humiliated by his appearance, received confidence to face the world. There came pilgrims too, who simply wanted to know the future.

Before the coming of Buddhism, the Emperor was the principal dreamer and incubation of his dreams was part of his religious duties. His palace contained a special dream hall equipped with an incubating bed known as a Kamudoko. Once, when a terrible plague threatened his people the Emperor Sujin lay upon his Kamudoko in search of an answer which would help his people. This he received when his god Amonon Ushi appeared to him in his dream, telling him how to avert the calamity that was speedily sweeping the land.

The Dreams of Native Peoples

Native Americans recognized the value of their dreams in helping them live peacefully together. The Huron and the Iroquois held regular dream festivals which lasted several days or even weeks, depending on the material collected. By pooling their dreams a distinct pattern emerged and this they used to help construct future tribal policy.

The Maoris in New Zealand and the Zulus in South Africa still pay particular attention to the pooling of dreams and their dream interpreters are appropriately called Head Men! Eskimos from the Hudson Bay, and the Patani people as far away as Malaysia share the belief that during sleep the soul leaves the body and experiences in a special dream world. They also think it is very dangerous to wake anyone suddenly, lest his spirit may not have time to return to his body and so might be trapped for ever in limbo.

The Temiar tribe, part of the Senois in Malaysia, are still profoundly influenced both by the interpretation and the manipulation of dreams. Their children are taught the importance of dreams from an early age and are encouraged to confront any bad spirits in their nightmares in order to master them before they grow up. As adults they pool their dream experiences, which they believe collectively reflect the future. Crimes and violence are unheard of, and as a society they are considered to be the most democratic and well-adjusted people on earth today.

These non-violent, self-reliant people were discovered by H. D. Noone in 1931 and since then they have intrigued Western sociologists with their peaceful, balanced way of life. What so impressed Noone was the way they lived according to their own natural law. 'Where a man has given his labour he has a share of the harvest, though each man received not in proportion to his skill and labour, but according to his needs,' he said. Here seems to be the very essence of Karl Marx's dream for humanity where he suggested that 'each man should work to his full ability and take according to his needs.'

Collective dreaming still takes place in Corsica. Villagers run their own affairs with the help of their dreams. As of old, they first concentrate on the problem, then dream about it. Next morning, many have had similar dreams relating to that which they need to understand. Without knowing anything about this custom, many holiday-makers on the island have discovered that, on waking, the whole family have had very similar dreams. It is as if a collective psyche takes over in the night and telepathically transmits a particular scene to those sleeping nearby, and then each person dreams of this in their own way.

ARTFUL DREAMING

'We are such stuff as dreams are made on,' Shakespeare says, and in the great literature, art, drama and music of our past we find many examples of the power and inspirational force of dreams. Poets, writers and artists throughout the ages have employed their dreams as mines of information on every subject under the sun, inspiring them to reflect on the profound psychological and paradoxical nature of man.

Expressing the confrontation of repressed savagery and open benevolence present within, we find literary revelations of the fears of hell, visions of horror and aspects of one's darker unknown self – never better summed up than by Plato in *The Republic* where he says, 'In all of us, even in good men, there is a lawless wild-beast nature which peers out in sleep.'

The symbolic paradise dream, set in a personal garden of delight, was another common theme, seen and written about in terms of compensation and wish-fulfilment. Tennyson's initial poems were filled with nocturnal landscapes inhabited by unapproachable maidens and nightingales, all seen and heard in a dream, and Keats with his dream gardens intruded regularly into 'some untrodden region of the mind'. Throughout the work of Shakespeare run themes and references to sleep and dreams, conveying those states of reality and illusion between which we so often find ourselves trapped. In fact, Coleridge, in his lectures on Shakespeare, insisted that the only way to understand the Bard's message was to interpret his plays as one would a series of images and ideas created and embodied in a dream.

Coleridge himself experienced many creative dreams and the most fruitful of them was his famous Kubla Khan. In a lonely Somerset farmhouse Coleridge was suffering from a slight indisposition that caused him to sleep for several hours. During this time a series of images and sentences came to him, and on waking he instantly began to write them all down, word for word. Unfortunately, he was interrupted by a man from Porlock who called on business, and as a result he lost several lines which he was never able to recall. In this we see the importance of recording a dream not only immediately on waking but without interruption, too!

Charles Lutwidge Dodgson, better known as Lewis Carroll, was first and foremost a mathematician but in his famous story, *Alice in Wonderland*, he has Alice falling into her own dream world by entering a rabbit hole. Adventures and fears experienced throughout this story are hardly child-ish passing fancies nor are they really intended to amuse young minds, for this wonderland, full of outrageous characters, conundrums, surprises, threats and disap-pointments represents and relates to the mature, not the immature or infantile mind. Profound psychological and psychic observations disguised as reality and expeditions into other dimensions are all thrown into the melting pot of this fabulously symbolic dream.

In his book *Across the Plains*, Robert Louis Stevenson described how complete stories came to him during sleep. Each night he would pick up the fantasy-thread where he had left it the night before and carry on from there.

Graham Greene told an audience in 1981 that his books wrote themselves in the dead of the night. Apparently, he would wake up four or five times to record outlines of dreams that later formed the basis of his novels. 'If I'm really working I re-read what I've written during the day before I go to bed and the problems are solved in my sleep.' He also went on to say that he kept a dream diary in which he recorded insights and story lines offered up by his unshackled mind!

Many inventors have to thank their dreams for their unique observations and discoveries, which later contributed to the development of our society and our way of life. In the 19th century a man called Elias Howe dreamed of men throwing spears and each spear had an eye-shaped hole at its tip. On waking he immediately knew that he had solved the problem of where to put the hole in the needle in his latest invention. It was the sewing machine.

Biblical and historical dreams have provided artists with exciting subjects to paint since at least the 11th century but it was not until the surrealist movement came along that dreams were psychologically captured in essence and in feeling. Surrealism, the name given to an artistic group in France in 1924, endeavoured to express dreams, the action of the unconscious mind, on to canvas. Although nightmares were no stranger to the imagination of the artist, Goya in particular excelling in this respect, none had tried to convey the atmosphere and symbolic message of the dream-experience until this time. 'Surrealism is based on a belief in the omnipotence of the dream,' said André Breton, often called the Pope of the Surrealist movement.

Salvador Dali's paintings, with titles like 'The Persistence of Memory', 'The Birth of Liquid Desires', 'The Spectre of Sex Appeal' and 'The Great Masturbator', depicting melting telephones and furniture, watches, crutches, barren beaches, starved embryos and limp fig-ures eerily produce appropriate, dreamlike atmospheres of general dis-ease, un-ease and obsession. In contrast, Max Ernst, with his 'Robing of the Bride' and 'The Eye of Silver', fills his scenes with forests, blazing suns, bird-headed women, rocks towering to the sky, silent swamps and mysterious figures all very much in keeping with the more archetypal imagery dreams sometimes possess.

Other artists in this group went on to paint anxiety dreams, portraying strong feelings of fear and terror in one form or another. Hypnagogic dreams were a popu-lar subject, too, showing images falling half-way between sleep and the waking state. Here to stay, surrealism certainly opened the door on our inner world, and in so doing contributed in its own way towards a better understanding of art, ourselves and, of course, dreams too, for dreams are very much like paintings.

Probably the greatest genius the world has known was 'the man who knew everything'; Leonardo da Vinci. An outstanding figure not only of the Renaissance, but before and since that time, he was an artist of rare power, and a pioneering scientist as well. His explorations were as diverse as anatomy, botany, geology, meteorology, physics, mathematics, geometry and music. His architectural drawings explored design problems in buildings, harbours, irrigation systems and canals, and his inventions were futuristic to say the least. These included sketches of submarines, diving suits, tanks, parachutes, flying machines, machine guns and cluster bombs, all at least 400 years before their time.

A genius is a visionary and a visionary is a dreamer. The difference between the da Vincis of this world and others is that they can pluck a thought or an idea that comes to them in the still of the night, in a dream and create from it reality. To them the true world is their inner world. Above all, they are good listeners, not only to other people but to that small, quiet voice within.

Dreams of the famous and infamous throughout the ages have without doubt helped to make history and shape our present way of life. In essence, however, their dreams are no different in any way from our dreams. We all have prophetic dreams, warning dreams and inspirational dreams just as they did, but we do not always accept them as sources of power and original thought. Recognize them, however, and immediately they step forward and begin to put our house, the mansion of our soul, in order. But we must first learn to dream.

CHAPTER TWO

OUR DREAMING PRESENT: THE SCIENCE OF SLEEP AND DREAMS

At the beginning of the 20th century, physiologists discovered that nerves and muscles, including the heart muscle, gave off electrical impulses. By the late 1920s they had found that the scalp also gave off similar wave motions. These, it was deduced, came from the brain and they were given the names Alpha and Beta waves. Since this time, Delta, Theta, Mu, Gamma, Vertex, Spike and 'k' brain waves have been identified as well. To obtain tracings of these waves, electrodes are attached to places on the body and head where internal activity is best picked up; these are then intensified and transformed into wave motions which are penned onto graph paper or projected onto an oscilloscope. These recordable physiological impulses and patterns are known as biofeedback data.

With the refinement of electronics came more and more detailed recordings of the brain's activity, and by the 1950s two distinct sleep states, dreaming and non-dreaming, had been recognized.

By the 1960s virtually every researcher used his own pet name for dreaming and non-dreaming sleep. These included 'deep and light', 'active and quiet', 'quiet and active', 'desynchronized and synchronized', 'high and low', and the most popular at the time, 'paradoxical and orthodox'.

NREM and REM Sleep States

Eventually it was noticed that rapid eye movements were associated with visual dreaming, so non-dreaming and dreaming sleep were referred to as non-REM or NREM, and REM sleep states.

Early experiments carried out on sleeping volunteers in the 1960s used seven electrodes, and much the same technique is still used today. Electrodes 1, 2 and 3 recorded cortical activity from the brain; 4 and 5 recorded eye movement; 6 recorded tone over the front of the neck and 7 recorded the heartbeat. The first surprise came when the subject closed his eyes. The cortical brain waves changed completely, as if in readiness for sleep. During sleep itself it was observed that the EEG could be divided into six distinct types which they labelled stages *A, B, C, D, E* and *F*.

It was the characteristic 'rapid eye movement' in Stage F that eventually became known as the REM sleep state.

During the night we progress through a series of sessions each lasting approximately 90 minutes. Throughout these the NREM and REM states alternate. We begin at stage 1 with NREM sleep and then move into further NREM stages 2, 3, 4 and 5. These are then followed by a phase of REM dreaming. It is this pattern that is repeated four, five or even six times each night, depending on how much sleep we need. As we move towards morning, however, NREM sleep decreases and REM sleep increases. This accounts for the fact that we remember the dreams we have early in the morning best, for it is just before we wake up that we have experienced our longest dreaming session.

The labelling of non-dreaming sleep, however, may not be quite as cut and dried as the terms suggest. Dream laboratory observations show that during the NREM sleep state there is still plenty of brain activity going on, so maybe it is a question of defining types of dreams more than types of sleep.

Perhaps during NREM sleep we are sorting out our outer mundane problems, but in REM sleep we are dealing with inner symbolic matters. This was, in fact, confirmed to some degree back in the 1960s when the belief was that paradoxical sleep, now called REM sleep, produced the recall of more exciting, psychic adventures, whilst orthodox sleep, now called NREM sleep, referred to everyday events.

It is in the level of sleep recognized as F, that is, deep REM sleep, that eye movement is greatest. It is known that visual dreaming takes place during these phases but what was not realized until recently was that when those in NREM phases were awakened, they too thought they were dreaming. Subjects who were constantly awoken during the night (in particular during REM sleep which meant they were deprived of visual dreaming), became irritable, nervous, bad tempered and behaved out of character generally. It can, therefore, be concluded that we sleep so that we can dream.

What Is Sleep?

In attempting to understand sleep and the brain, they have been compared with many things, including radio broadcasting, the telephone, television and now the computer. Using computer language researchers say we are 'on-line' for two-thirds of a day and 'off-line' for the other third. When we are 'off-line' during sleep our brain, like that of a computer, is not idle or resting but is busy reassessing, classifying and updating the day's input. It then abandons all irrelevant outdated information. Our dreams, according to these theorists, are like the siftings from this abandoning process.

Even assuming this analogy to be correct, it is still only a fragment of the whole concept of sleep and we shall need a lot more than man-made electronic gadgets to discover the real truth. It is, however, true that we often wake in the morning and find our problems have lessened and even been solved, and we sometimes come up with original ideas too, all due perhaps to mental reassessment, computer-fashion. Past memories, however, are not obliterated as in the case of the computer clearance system. They are retained forever. Sleep is, among other things, undoubtedly a great restorative although not in the way earlier researchers once thought. Energy accumulated during sleep is on a different level from energy stored from food and that acquired from physical rest; it has the power to heal us both physically and mentally.

PHYSICAL CHANGES DURING SLEEP

Many things do happen to us physically as well as mentally when we are asleep and, what is more, these changes are undoubtedly responsible for some of our dreams, nightmares and experiences during sleep. Take, for example, that feeling of suddenly stepping off a kerb, the shock of which wakes us with a start. This happens in the early stages of sleep and is due to a reflex action which produces sudden muscular contractions. This is called a myoclonic jerk. The sensation of falling, not to be confused with a dream of flying and weightlessness, also happens in early light sleep and arises from our mental appreciation of that twilight stage between waking and sleeping.

Another sleep experience which is physical in origin is that of seeing a flash of brilliant light, hearing a shot or sensing something like an explosion inside the head. All these are thought to result from electrical stimulation of the occipital region of the brain, in turn due to a build-up of static electricity accumulated in the larger muscles, mainly the limbs. This is then discharged in the form of a self-induced electric shock from the body to the head. As startling as this surge of energy is, it has been known to have beneficial healing effects and is apparently responsible for some remarkable cures.

Paralysis is an unpleasant sensation we sometimes experience in sleep and this is not a dream, nor is it imagination. It is very real indeed. The reason for this is that during sleep the muscular reflexes associated with our limbs completely disappear with the result that we are literally unable to move. When this is incorporated into a dream, as it often is, it is usually one where we are being chased but cannot move!

OUTER AND INNER DISTURBANCES

Outer and inner stimuli, not sufficient to awaken us immediately, are sometimes incorporated into our dreams. With ingenuity our economical dreaming mind makes full use of external noises as well as internal physical disturbances and weaves them into meaningful dreams which offer messages to be thought out and interpreted on waking.

When it comes to dreams using inner stimuli we have only to think of the old wives' tale about eating cheese late at night and this giving us nightmares. The truth is that a late-night snack, and not only one of cheese, can give some people indigestion. The aggravation of the stomach is then used as a basis for a disturbing but nevertheless warning dream, and with good reason. The message from this is clearly telling the dreamer not to eat last thing at night, or else!

When a pain is acute enough it wakes us up so that we can do something about it at once, but if it is milder and goes on for some time, it can become the theme for a healing dream, in which case a remedy will be given.

FALSE AWAKENINGS

One reason for believing that we wake up in the middle of the night and see strange things in the bedroom like green monsters, weird animals and long-departed relatives is that we are actually dreaming that we are awake! This is so real that it is hard, if not impossible, to convince ourselves it simply was a dream!

A DREAM WITHIN A DREAM

Just as we sometimes dream we are awake, conversely we can dream we are asleep and dreaming. This produces a dream within a dream. One explanation is that in such dreams we reach deeper levels of awareness, but since these dreams are often of a mundane nature, apparently of little significance and no more revealing than other dreams, there is no evidence to support this theory. The point of them may, therefore, simply be to emphasize the necessity of looking deeply into certain problems and situations.

FALLING

Falling through space is a sensation we often experience soon after 'falling asleep' or 'dropping off' to sleep. Not surprisingly, our unconscious associates this with the real thing and so incorporates it into a dream event, so that it seems that we are, for example, falling through space or dropping down a well.

There are also 'falling' dreams which occur long after we have fallen asleep. Our dreaming mind creates these for a purpose. Not surprisingly, they offer a message telling us that we fear we are 'falling from grace', 'being dropped', 'will fall upon hard times' or have to go through an ordeal that will 'bring us down'. There is an old wives' tale associated with this dream which says that if you reach the bottom you will die. This is not true. Many have landed safely but we do usually wake up before we get there.

BEING CHASED

The feeling of *being chased* by someone or something, yet unable to run away or move, is as mentioned associated with the muscles in our limbs. As with the myoclonic jerk, our unconscious awareness of not being able to move is often transformed into a scene in which we are rooted to the spot and cannot get away from whatever it is that is pursuing us. Sometimes the pursuer represents an aspect of the dreamer's own hostile tendencies, and sometimes it is the hostile tendencies of others. If, however, we can consciously identify the thing that chases us during the night, and can turn to face it during the day, it will no longer haunt our consciousness or our unconscious.

WALKING AND TALKING IN OUR SLEEP

Sleep walking, known too as somnambulism, is an attempt to externalize a dream by putting it into action. Children do this far more than adults, probably because they are less inhibited and more agile. Most of us grow out of the habit but if an occasion arises which is severely distressing, we may, like Shakespeare's Lady Macbeth, actively express the nightmare in this way.

Talking in our sleep is similar, in cause, to sleep walking. It is an attempt to consciously express a dream verbally. It is possible to carry on a conversation with a sleeping person who is inclined to talk in their sleep, and to receive replies, but these are sometimes unintelligible.

When we are under mental pressure or we are not well physically we are more likely to sleep walk or talk. Most of the time we do not come to harm when we sleep walk but this is not always the case. Some somnambulists awake and find themselves in real danger, so it is a practice which should not be encouraged. Precautions should, therefore, be taken, especially where stairs and open windows are concerned.

TELEPATHY

Telepathic communication often takes place during dreams, usually spontaneously. It has been found that when we dream of someone we have not thought about for some time, there is a good chance that they have reciprocated and likewise dreamed of us. Two communicants do not necessarily have to be in harmony for this to happen, but telepathic links are more likely to occur when a close emotional relationship exists.

Sometimes a telepathic message is one of pain, fear and death. An example of this is the dreamer who awoke at 2 am from a dream in which she saw her father holding his hand over his heart and at the same time felt a stabbing pain in her own chest. Next morning she telephoned her father's home and was told that he had died during the night from a heart attack. This happened at 2 am, the precise moment she had the dream.

Experiencing pain or unpleasant events which do not relate directly to the dreamer is known as 'sympathetic dreaming'. Telepathic transference of a strong feeling or emotion is one explanation for those dreams which relate to the experiences of others. Such dreams are not prophetic; prophetic dreams reveal that which has not yet occurred.

TELEPORTATION

Teleportation is projection to a distant bedside, where the dreamer in that bed actually sees the dream visitor standing there. This vision may be a false awakening or it may appear in a dream, but either way, evidence exists that this experience does take place. A mother who dreamed her daughter in Australia was seriously ill had this confirmed when she telephoned her next morning. She also discovered that her daughter had seen her mother standing by the bedside. Her daughter had been asleep during the day, so the times of the two dream experiences coincided exactly.

This phantom vision, the ghost of a living person, is known as a 'fetch'. Although most teleportations occur between those closely related, it is not always so. The experience of Tudor Pole, a well-known radio broadcaster, archaeologist, writer and philosopher in the 1930s, was a classic example. When excavating in Egypt he was taken ill with a severe fever. One night, as he restlessly dreamed, he thought he heard a tap on the cabin door. He awoke, or so he believed, and standing by his bed was a doctor dressed in a black cloak and wearing a top hat. The hat fascinated him because he could see right through it. The doctor placed this on a small table then proceeded to tell Tudor Pole that he was in practice in Britain but on some nights he travelled all over the world to visit those who needed his help. He then left, after giving the patient a special potion, which he drank. Next morning, Tudor Pole had recovered completely. The sequel to this was that when Tudor Pole returned to Britain, he appealed on BBC radio for this ghostly healer to come forward and, as a result, a Scottish doctor contacted him and confirmed that he did, in fact, travel during his sleep to those in need.

FLYING

Flying dreams, known too as a form of astral projection, are experienced by seven out of ten people, at least once in their life. It is a most exhilarating feeling and few, if any, find it frightening. By using your arms like wings it is possible to rise above the ground and travel beyond the bedroom into the street, soar above the treetops and out into the country. It is even possible to be transported to faraway places and, as proof of this, bring back information that could not have been received in any other way. One explanation is that during sleep the spirit leaves the body. The practical belief is that such a dream reflects our inherited memory when, according to Darwin's theory, our ancestors were birds. Psychologically, it is explained as a form of depersonalization. These, however, are merely words to describe an experience none of us truly understands.

Whichever of these theories is correct, if indeed any, it still remains that there is a close link between flying dreams of this nature and teleportation. A further revelation is that a person who can fly in their sleep is rarely of a depressive nature. Symbolically, this makes sense because in reality flying dreams show that the dreamer wishes, or indeed is able to rise above his or her problems. They may also denote a desire to be free from a mundane situation that ties the dreamer to a life that is restrictive.

DREAMS AND OBJECTS

Without a doubt the most common object about which we dream is a house or building. Forty per cent of these dreams concentrate on the whole structure, and these vary from a small flat to a rambling mansion or even to an ugly, sprawling factory. Twenty-five per cent are centred around one room which may be a bedroom, kitchen, dining room, lounge, attic, cellar, office or school-room. Fifteen per cent involve stairs and corridors, eleven per cent focus on doors and exits generally and nine per cent highlight windows.

Dreams of streets and gardens, followed by dreams of travelling by car, train, bus, horse, bicycle, aeroplane and walking on foot are next in line, with UFOs and space journeys as runners-up. Swimming, playing games, watching a play or film and fighting also feature prominently, with men having five times as many hostile dreams as women. Both males and females, however, experience an equal share of sex dreams.

When it comes to dreaming in colour, only twenty-nine per cent of 3,000 dreamers asked thought they did; although possibly everyone does and only this percentage remembers or notices it. The memory of colour, like a dream itself, fades quickly on waking. Concerning the time a dream lasts, for years it was believed that they were over in fractions of a second, but now it is thought they last for anything from a few seconds to over 30 minutes.

HOW MUCH SLEEP DO WE NEED?

Babies begin life by sleeping 75 per cent of a 24-hour day, although this takes some believing, knowing some babies. The reverse of this time-scale often seems nearer the truth in reality. However, when they are asleep they spend most of their time in REM dreaming sleep, and this they do even before they are born. The interesting question arises, 'Of what are they dreaming?' If they have no experience of the outer world, how on earth could they possibly dream of anything, let alone become excited, happy, angry and even extremely amused at such an innocent age? Whilst many baby-smiles are due to wind, that deep-throated chuckle reminiscent of an experienced old man or woman, heard only in the first three weeks of life, is not. Could this be a sign of some merry private joke? And what of those incredibly bad childhood nightmares arising from terrifying thoughts far removed from the security of warm nurseries and all-loving parental care? Difficult birth experiences and bad memories from this are among the answers put forward, as are reincarnation theories.

Turning to adults, they have 7 hours 20 minutes sleep each night on average, but this is very much an individual matter. As we grow older we tend to need less sleep. It was also found that men sleep more than women; extroverts sleep more than introverts, and overweight people sleep more than thin people.

It is impossible to have too much sleep, but if prolonged bouts do occur it usually means we are either catching up on lost dreaming and generally recharging ourselves, or we are ill. Most illnesses require extra sleep, for it is during this that self-healing takes place. This is why children go to sleep the moment they feel off-colour, irrespective of the time of day. Unfortunately, as adults we cannot always do this, although it would save a lot of trouble if we did.

INSOMNIA

We tend to worry too much about not sleeping and although deprivation of this is exhausting, to become anxious only adds to the problems which caused it in the first place.

Anxiety, and the complete reverse from this, joyous elation, both inhibit sleep. The reason for this is that in each of these states our mind is over-active and will not switch off when the day is done. Excitement-triggered insomnia, however, is fleeting, like a dream itself, but unfortunately that which is caused by worry tends to become chronic and soon turns into a regular nightmare!

Sleeping Tips
Reading in bed is an excellent way to divert and concentrate our thoughts on something other than problems. Making sure our hands and feet are warm helps too and so does the adoption of a breathing pattern similar to that of the breathing rhythm in sleep. By breathing in to

the count of two, and out to the count of three, we are
imitating this rhythm and in so doing invite and pave the
way for that oft elusive state! Visualization, the creation
of imaginary scenes in our mind, is another excellent way
of inviting sleep.

Whether we realize it or not we all have the ability to solve our problems in two different ways, on two distinctly different levels of understanding. When we are awake we use our intellect and reasoning powers, but when we are asleep our inspiration and symbolic vision takes over. Figuratively, these contributions are from our heads and from our hearts. The power of dreams which provides the inspirational visions works spontaneously, so we are, for the most part, unaware of the unique role it has played in helping us. 'Sleep on it' is advice readily given to those faced with difficult decisions and apparently insoluble situations, and most of us have experienced the benefit of doing this. Often we have gone to sleep with fears rampaging through our heads, yet on waking in the morning find to our intense relief that the cloud has lifted and hope has returned. And this improvement in our affairs, thanks to our dreaming minds, we usually take for granted.

It is, however, the blending of these two aspects, the intellectual and the inspirational, the head and the heart, that gives us not only original answers to ordinary problems, but enables us, if we really want to, to make unique discoveries as well.

One inspirational dream that revolutionized the world was that of Fredrich August von Kekule, a professor of chemistry in Ghent a hundred years ago. He was having difficulty understanding the molecular structure of a certain substance when, one day, he dozed and had a dream. In this he saw atoms gambolling before his eyes. There were smaller groups which kept in the background, and in the foreground, with the acute vision peculiar to dreams, he distinguished larger structures forming strange configurations. These were in long chains, twisting and turning in snake-like fashion. Suddenly, he was astounded to see one snake seize its own tail and mockingly form a circle. On waking it dawned on him that the circle formed by the snake symbolized the missing link in his researches. By transforming this scene into logic, he discovered it represented the ring theory underlying the constitution of benzene. In essence, he had discovered the complex mixture of hydrocarbons underlying the synthesis of petrol from oil.

From sleep and dreams come our energy and our inspirations too, which in no way could we receive from intellect alone. Above all, we receive encouragement and hope for the future.

'Sleep', as Shakespeare so wisely put it, 'is the balm for hurt minds, nature's great second course.'

PSYCHOLOGICAL AND PSYCHIC
APPROACHES TO DREAMS

For all the sleeping hours clocked up by the human race and the untold millions of dreams experienced over the years, it is a sobering thought to realize that we understand dreams less today than our ancestors did two, three or even four thousand years ago. We may think we are covering new ground when we use dreams to solve problems and try to understand ourselves through them, but this is nothing new. It was, however, Sigmund Freud, the father of psychiatry, who altered the way people thought about their dreams and themselves by introducing the psychoanalytical or psychological approach.

THE PSYCHOLOGICAL APPROACH

Sigmund Freud (1856–1939) certainly did not believe dreams to be ramblings from uncontrolled minds, but saw them as scenes from an unconscious state underlying conscious awareness. Originally he thought they were reflections relating to conscious experiences, since he recognized in them symptoms of hysteria, abnormal behaviour and even physical disease, projected symbolically. Hysteria, an abnormal behaviour pattern, and physical symptoms are symbolic in themselves anyway, since they are secondary effects from a primary cause. For example, a rash is a physical effect but at the same time a symbol reflecting its underlying cause; and on a mental level the person who vomits easily may not be able to digest unpalatable facts, so this, in turn, symbolizes the cause.

By encouraging his patients to go on talking at length about their dreams and the off-theme thoughts they provoked, Freud perfected his chain-reaction technique now popularly known as the Free Association of Ideas. However irrational the ideas were, avoidance of the truth seemed to Freud to be apparent by its absence. From this came his theory of repression and wish-fulfilment. After formulating the association of ideas, Freud tracked down what he called Habitual Complexes, later described by Jung as 'those tender spots of the psyche which react most to stimulus or disturbance'. These complexes are walled-up innermost secrets which we now know can be reached and freed by methods other than through the free association of ideas in dreams. The inkblot test devised by Rorschach serves as an excellent stimulus for this, as indeed does any irregular shape or object, and in this lies the secret of crystal gazing and scrying.

> Leonardo da Vinci wrote, 'It should not be hard for you to stop something and look into the stains on the wall or the ashes in the fire or the clouds in the sky or even mud, in which you will find really marvellous ideas.'

Freud went to great lengths to maintain his theory that all dreams represented a wish fulfilment. 'The fulfilment of a wish is its only purpose and even dreams with painful contents are to be analysed as fulfilment wishes,' he urged. One difficulty, however, was for him to explain satisfactorily fear and anxiety in wish-fulfilment terms.

The professor also noticed 'day residues' in dreams which were all mixed up with memories. This observation, along with results he achieved with hysterics under hypnosis, eventually led him to the development of and treatment through psychoanalysis. By 1893 he expressed his conclusions, declaring that extreme physical symptoms recognized in hysteria were caused not by pathological changes but by emotional psychic energy. This was converted into physical symptoms so that the nervous condition became the 'conversion neurosis'. Later, he described this psychic energy as being sexual in nature, and his work with dreams convinced him that all the symbols found in these were projections from repressed sexual hang-ups, laced with guilt.

Carl Gustav Jung (1875–1961) was Freud's pupil. He disagreed with Freud's belief that sexual repression was the underlying stimulating cause of dreams, and put forward his own insightful theories that have helped us to understand the psyche.

Jung believed that dreams had a special purpose of their own which indicated an underlying idea or intention which was not apparent on the surface. He began, therefore, to pay attention to the actual form of a dream. This technique was diametrically opposed to Freud's free association, for it was intended to exclude, not encourage, irrelevant thoughts. Jung, like the soothsayers of old, recognized in dreams powers well beyond our personal traits.

THE ANIMA AND ANIMUS

Jung researched ancient beliefs and dreams extensively, and came to believe that the pattern of the universe was one of duality. He believed that this quality existed within individuals as well as in nature. The feminine element in the male character Jung called *anima*, and the masculine element in the female character he called the *animus*. Throughout life we undergo a process of what Jung called *individuation*, whereby these two aspects of the self, the feminine and the masculine, attempt to unite.

Signs, Symbols, Archetypes and the Collective Unconscious

If signs and symbols are not Jungian in origin, archetypes and the collective unconscious certainly are. The definitions Jung gave to signs, symbols and archetypes are also unique. 'The sign is always less than the concept it represents while the symbol always stands for something more than its obvious and immediate meaning. Archaic remnants I call Archetypes or primordial images.'

A symbol hints at something not yet known and it is this that occurs spontaneously in dreams. Symbols happen, they are not inventions of the conscious mind, and as such are our main source of knowledge in this respect, occurring in dreams, daydreams, visions and psychic phenomena.

The concept of archetypes is very important in the understanding of dream symbology for it explains why some dreams have a universal meaning which applies to everyone, and why others are purely personal and concern the dreamer only.

Archetypes appear in dreams, daydreams, visions and phenomena too, again without the dreamer having prior knowledge of their existence, but whereas an archetype is a symbol, a symbol is not necessarily an archetype. One explanation for archetypes in dreams is that primordial images form part of an inherited ancestral memory. Just as we inherit physical characteristics going back to primitive biological life-patterns, so too do we possess primary mental essences arising from a collective psyche. An archetype is not, therefore, a mythological image, although it is often mistaken and represented as such; the mythological image is, in turn, a symbol of an underlying force. In this lies the mystery and meaning of the ancient gods, each of whom symbolized and represented a different force and principle of nature and the universe.

The source from which all this stemmed Jung called the *collective unconscious* but, again, this was not an entirely new concept. As he himself said, 'It is the foundation of what the ancients called the sympathy of all things.' Others might equally well call it the Akashic records, but whatever name we give it, it does seem that from this universal reservoir there flows a stream of powerful cosmic memories which we contact, or perhaps they contact us, through our dreams.

If the main symbol in a dream was, say, an apple, then the Freudian free association of ideas trail would go like this: 'Apple, pears, stairs, bedroom, bed and sex.'

Alternatively, the Jungian treatment of the apple symbol would be more like this: 'Apple, knowledge, wisdom, but what about the apple? Apple, food for thought. Apple, tree of life, family tree, family problems. Back again to the apple; temptation in the Garden of Eden.' By applying the meanings directly associated with the symbol, the underlying meaning would eventually be revealed. Jung also favoured a series of dreams, associating one with the next, to unravel his patients' problems, whereas Freud concentrated on one at a time as isolated incidents.

THE PSYCHIC APPROACH

The dreamers of old, who attributed their nightly experiences to external forces, took the psychic approach to dreams. Undoubtedly, they believed God and His angels, the gods and goddesses of nature, various spirits and the discarnate entities who helped them were at man's disposal and could be contacted through dreams when necessary. In those days they deliberately invoked these influences by incubating their dreams, but even without doing this, psychic dreams can and do occur spontaneously. When they do they are usually recognized as great spiritual truths and enlightening experiences which have the power to alter a destiny, solve a problem or heal physically or mentally. Unfortunately, there are also other external influences and forces around which are far from beneficial.

The dream Adolf Hitler is said to have experienced during the First World War certainly altered the course of history. Apparently he was sleeping in a bunker with many other war-wearied soldiers in 1917, when he had a most disturbing nightmare. In this, debris and molten earth fell upon him, crushing and suffocating him. He awoke in a terrible fright and ran outside into the cold night air, thankful that it had all been a bad dream. As he stood there, a shell hit the bunker, killing every sleeping occupant. To Hitler, this was divine providence. God, he believed, had saved him to save the Fatherland. This shows yet again the effect, for good or ill, that dreams can have on the whole of humanity.

Psychic attacks via dreams are more likely when we are ill, particularly if we have a fever. The possible reason for this is that our aura, that protective energy-field around us, is weakened to the extent that it is easily breached. It is this aspect of dreaming that leads us into the parapsychological field where there is still much to be explained. The ultimate goal, if one is to work in this field of experience, must surely be in the understanding of lucid dreams, where we have a degree of control over them.

Lucid Dreams

Dreams reflect life as a whole, from the ordinary to the extraordinary. To single out any one aspect of dreaming, psychic or otherwise, presupposes that one facet of life is more important than another which, of course, it is not.

Interest in the beliefs of those such as the mystic Mexican Don Juan, through the writings of Carlos Castaneda, exemplifies an emphasis on psychic dreams, for Don Juan saw them as aids to the development of psychic and mental powers. To increase these powers, he said, one had to become conscious whilst dreaming, and then learn how to manipulate the dream. This brings us to lucid dreaming, which until relatively recently was thought to be so rare and unimportant that Freud, Jung and other renowned psychologists virtually ignored it. When, however, a group of average people, not selected dreamers with any interest in dreams, were asked if they ever had a dream in which they knew they were dreaming, 73 per cent said they had. This shows that lucid dreams are far more frequent than the experts previously thought, and their importance lies in the fact that they form a link between the psychological, psychic and mystical aspects of the mind.

The term 'lucid dreaming' was first used at the beginning of the 20th century by a Dutchman named van Eeden, himself a prolific lucid dreamer. Sometimes he found that these dreams were preceded two or three nights before with flying dreams, but the main distinguishing feature of a lucid dream is that we know, without a shadow of a doubt, that we are dreaming. The scene is very real in one sense, but the improbable and the impossible are sometimes there too, although at the time the situation or events do not seem to be out of place or odd.

Dr Keith Hearne from Hull has made an extensive study of lucid dreams. In his dream laboratory he instigated a new method which establishes communication between the sleeping subject and the dream investigator. Another aspect of his work was directed towards actively encouraging lucid dreams by producing an external stimulus from a special apparatus called 'a dream machine'. Apart from discovering further electro-physiological information which showed the type of sleep and brain-waves associated with lucid dreaming, Dr Hearne also found that these dreams have both psychological and psychic implications far beyond those recognized in dreams generally by Freud and Jung.

Within the bounds of lucid dreams there are many aspects of awareness. In one we may find ourselves saying, 'This is ridiculous. It can't possibly happen so I must be dreaming.' You could say this is the analytical way of looking at a dream when actually dreaming, the counterpart of which is that waking experience where, when something nasty happens, we say hopefully, 'I don't believe it. I will wake up in a minute and find it is a ghastly dream.' Happily we wake up from lucid nightmares – unfortunately there is no such escape from the daytime experience!

Apart from this kind of conscious rationalization during a dream, this awareness or lucidity can have psychic associations too, but unless the dreamer recognizes and understands these the experience is simply filed away among, no doubt, other valuable but wasted dreams. It is, therefore, no understatement to say that the latent potential in a lucid dream is enormous, but the secret of releasing this potential lies in being able to control the dream itself. If we can do this then we can begin to have greater control over our own lives and may even be able to alter our course of destiny, if necessary. This introduces the question of free will, which most of us believe we have, at least to some degree.

THE CONTROL OF DREAMS

The next stage beyond that of knowing we are dreaming is when we begin to control and manipulate a dream and make things happen that we want to happen. Just as we can control and create day-dream images, so too can we control and create a dream when asleep, but there are important distinctions between the two. During sleep our awareness is far more acute than when awake. On a scientific level this is registered as altered brain-wave patterns, and in practice it manifests itself as prophetic warnings and messages, healing, flashes of enlightenment and the ability to achieve feats well beyond our wildest dreams.

Since it is possible to control a lucid dream the implications are enormous. There is no reason why any one of us cannot use dreams in this way to help us along the often stony road through life. Problem-solving and self-healing, as well as many other personal goals, are well within our scope if we really want to make use of our incredible dream power.

THE CAUSE OF DREAMS

The inevitable question is, who or what initiates, designs and even decides that we need a particular dream, on a certain night, in the first place? In other words, what is the cause of dreams? Since appropriate dreams always come at the right time – and even before time in the case of prophetic dreams – chance can be ruled right out. Some theorists are content with their biological explanation of a physical cause; the psychologists remain satisfied with underlying psychological reasons; the psychics are happy in their conviction that discarnate beings and strange forces are responsible. Where does that leave us? The multiple choice of dream-producing stimuli coming from without, from within, from above and from who knows where else is most unsatisfactory, especially since all are so plausible in their own right. If, however, we take into account the law of cause and effect on a grand scale, it is possible to see that none of these is an explanation at all, nor a cause in itself. They are all effects.

From this standpoint it is clear that what is seen as a cause, say indigestion, is in fact only an effect, with the ensuing nightmare reflecting symbolically the symptoms and sufferings of an overstuffed stomach. By regressing this one stage, the reason for the gorging is found. A celebration dinner, arranged perhaps months ago, and from here the trail leads back and back in time, through events and associations until eventually childhood, babyhood and maybe even a time before that is reached. In this light the dream is no longer seen as the direct result of a physical cause; it is now simply an effect in a much longer chain of action and reaction. And psychological dreams conform in exactly the same way, showing, for example, the Freudian sexual cause to be nothing more than an effect, like a bead on the thread of life. No hang-up, sexual or otherwise, is ever an isolated cause in itself, in or out of a dream.

Prophetic dreams, where a scene clearly shows future events, appear to prove the exception to this rule, but they too fit into this pattern. It is not the succession of cause and effect that has altered, but our appreciation and perception of time. This is because we are conditioned to perceive time only in chronological order, but time has another, unconscious concept which has little or no place in our restricted three-dimensional world, so, in our waking state, it is suppressed. When it does get a look-in, however, we call it coincidence.

It is said that Julius Caesar, a prolific dreamer, was guided by his dreams. On the strength of a dream, in which he violated his own mother, he decided to take his army across the Rubicon, a small river running along the Cisalpine border. The result of this was that he had in fact invaded his own motherland, an action that led to war between Caesar and the Senate.

He may well have acted upon his own dreams, but he disregarded those of others, in particular one his wife Calpurnia had. According to Shakespeare, her dream warned Caesar of 'the Ides of March' (ie March 15th). If he had heeded this murderous portent, the tragedy would have been averted, and Calpurnia's dream would have remained a warning and not progressed into a prophecy.

The ancients knew all about time in both these contexts, calling them Chronos and Cairos to describe the difference between experiencing time (Chronos) and the appreciation of the quality of time (Cairos). Chronos is measured in seconds, minutes, days, years and centuries, thus giving us experiences in chronological order as we travel along life's highway. Alternatively, Cairos is actual participation within time itself, giving us those out-of-time, timeless moments. It is during Cairos that synchronistic events occur which we call coincidences.

Once we become aware of time in these ways, prophetic experiences in dreams need no further explanation – for past, present and future all exist and belong to the eternal now.

Returning to the ultimate cause of a dream, it seems to me that no single cause or stimulus can, therefore, possibly be isolated, other than that of ourselves. Experiences, influences, inheritances, environment, temperament, parents and ancestors all contribute to our individual destiny. Dreams, like mirrors, reflect all this – and more! Every dream event is linked in a different way, if we could but see it, so there is no cause as such, only effects. And if we could fully understand this linking pattern, we would discover not only the secret of dreaming but the secret of life itself. This, however, is a dream of the future, for the future.

CHAPTER THREE

THE LANGUAGE OF DREAMS

A dream interpreter is a dream analyst working entirely with dreams. As a dream analyst I do not discuss dreams with the dreamer – if I did it would, from my standpoint, amount to cheating! After all, by looking at a person and asking a few pertinent questions it is easy to learn all you need to know about him and his dream!

It is the dream that needs analysing, not the dreamer.

If one has a preconceived idea about the dreamer, this obviously colours and distorts the whole interpretation. Many letters I receive describing dreams are signed with initials only, so they might well be from a man or a woman, but this in no way alters the interpretation. Why should it?

MESSAGES FROM OURSELVES TO OURSELVES

Having interpreted over 12,000 dreams, I must confess to having paved yet another approach road to dreams. This one focuses attention completely on the dream itself, without knowledge or help from the dreamer. When searching for a reliable foundation upon which to build an interpretational framework, it seemed important that the first step should be to lay down concrete definitions, where possible. Obviously dreams are messages, but as we see from history, literature, religion and scientific investigations, no one is sure who sends them. Having considered this without much success, the answer came, not surprisingly, from a dream. In this I was looking and talking to myself in a mirror! On waking and on reflection (as it were!), it was abundantly clear that dreams were indeed messages, but from no one else other than ourselves. The more I looked at them this way, the more sure I was that they were unique creations which sometimes seemed to have been triggered by inner and outer stimuli which were incorporated into our dreams, but for which we were still the originators. The first definition had, therefore, to be that dreams were messages from ourselves to ourselves. From the psychological standpoint there are no holds barred when messages of self-truth are revealed in a dream, for the barrier between the conscious and unconscious is down. This explains how all those repressed urges, fears and long-lost memories come to light so effortlessly. But to limit dreams to the role of psychological policeman is to under-estimate them completely, for this is only one facet, important as it is, of many.

The Dreaming Mind

To bridge across gap between the conscious and unconscious minds I call The Dreaming Mind. In a way this is the dream itself but, whatever this link really is, it is there when we are awake as well as when we are asleep. If you think about it, when we mull over past memories or consciously conjure up thoughts for the future, two-way traffic starts up as we mentally pass back and forth between the conscious and unconscious. This bridge also accounts for day-dreaming, and those rare but remarkable visions which occur spontaneously and refuse to fit into logical reasoning. Day-dreams, visions, psychic phenomena and vivid imaginings, however, are not the same as dreams, although they all share certain characteristics.

TYPES OF DREAMS

The next step towards understanding dreams is to try to identify the different types of dreams, but this is not as easy as it sounds. There are so many, from fear dreams, wishful-thinking dreams, sad dreams, sex dreams, to a thousand and one other types. In fact, if you add virtually any adjective to the word 'dream' you have another type! Fortunately, two of my dreams came to the rescue at the appropriate time, and although neither of them produced startling messages as such, they revealed something else again.

In the first dream I was busy painting and wallpapering my kitchen, as I had actually done a few weeks before. It was as realistic as if I had actually been there, and apart from this nothing else happened. The other dream, that same night, was completely different. The setting was an unfamiliar house and I was searching in strange rooms for something among old, discarded furniture. It was impossible to describe either of these dreams as frightening, happy, sexy or anything else for that matter, yet they just had to be something! Both were set in houses, one familiar and one not, and I was the only person involved in each of them. Eventually it dawned on me that the first dream was a literal dream and the second was a symbolic dream. Here, then, were not just two types of dreams but two basic differences, or principles. From this it seemed logical to suppose that all dreams were either literal, symbolic, or a mixture of the two. Once having recognized this, then and only then could prefixes like fearful, warning, sexy, psychic or what have you, be added to identify and label them further as various types of dreams.

LITERAL DREAMS

Literal dreams reflect the outside world in a practical, unemotional and, as far as possible, intellectual way. They show literal scenes where problems and solutions can be seen and sorted out logically in the cold light of day, with the head, not the heart. It is not surprising that there is a high literal content in many dreams when we consider that children are taught from an early age to think clearly and without silly imaginings. Once conditioned like this, even the dreaming mind gives in and presents its offerings in the same literal vein.

Some people do not recognize the existence of literal dreams, so consequently try to give symbolic meanings where none is required. By reading mystery into them they complicate a straightforward dream and so miss the point, not to mention the message, completely. What we have to remember is that there are no symbols in literal dreams, only signs, and these are meant to be taken at face value.

Dogmatic intellectual thinkers tend to have literal, unimaginative dreams because this is the way they think and this is the only possible way they could accept a message from their dreams. This, of course, limits their vision, but once the dream-gates of perception are opened their literal dreams soon become interspersed with symbols representing hitherto unknown qualities, potential and originality.

Excellent examples of literal dreams can be found in the New Testament. In fact, most of the dreams in this part of the Bible are literal and give literal, practical messages. One of the best-documented accounts is given in Matthew 2: 11–12. Here we read how the three wise men took gifts to Bethlehem to give to the newborn King. Then in a dream one of them received the following warning: '"Return not to Herod"; and they departed for their country another way.'

A further example is found in the next verse which continues: 'And when they were departed an angel of the Lord appeared to Joseph in a dream saying "Arise and take the young child and his mother, and flee into Egypt and remain there until I bring you further word for Herod will seek the young child to destroy him."' When Herod was dead, Joseph received another dream as promised, telling him it was safe for him and his family to return to their native land.

These dreams did not have to be interpreted because their messages were self-explicit. What had to be done, however, was to heed the warnings and act upon the advice they gave.

ACTION-REPLAY DREAMS

Literal dreams then, reflecting and relating to the familiar world about us, faithfully reproduce scenes and people as they really are. They may recall past memories, show present situations or suggest future events, but one thing is certain and that is they are never sentimental. Vividly revived childhood events and memories which arise in dreams, for example, are not idle fantasies for old-times' sake, they are for a very good reason.

Rarely, if ever, do dreams go over past happenings simply for the heaven or hell of it. Reliving bad events allows the dreamer to see them differently in the hope of being able to accept or come to terms with whatever it is that is relived. If it is frightening or even sad, these dream experiences can 'innoculate' us mentally against the pain and anguish. On the other side of this coin there are the funny happenings repeated to show that laughter is the best medicine and that life has its lighter side. Passionate moments, too, are welcome action-replays, if only to reinforce or stoke up romantic feelings. The agony and the ecstasy of love dreams are stop-gaps for those who cannot be with the one they love, and if the heart rules exclusively in these, then so much the better!

Literal dreams are action-replays and can be compared with Saturday afternoon sport on television, where a re-run of events shows the scoring of a goal, the winning horse or the cricketer caught out. When looking at these action-replay shots for the second time we notice so much more than we did the first time around. So it is with action-replay dreams.

The purpose of these dreams, therefore, is to give us another chance to re-assess a particular incident or situation we did not fully understand at the time. If an experience was misconstrued at the time, it had wrong associations from the start, so consequently was filed away in the memory in the wrong place. In this we see shades of Freud's association of ideas, along with crossed wires and inevitable hang-ups, but by dreaming them over again as action-replays, we are given a wonderful opportunity to relive these events and see them for what they really are. This should enable us to set the record and our memory-filing system straight!

WARNINGS AND PROPHECIES

One example showing how this worked in practice came from a lady employed in a large open-plan office. In her dream she was sitting at her desk listening suspiciously to workmates talking and whispering about her. On waking she realized that her dream was an exact action-replay of what had happened the previous day but going over the dream, she discovered that as well as whispering, the women involved in this were huddled together as if looking down at something. Suddenly, the truth dawned on her. It was her birthday next day so could the conspiracy and secrecy possibly concern her birthday card and not her?

As well as showing the dreamer the truth about her paranoic character, this dream also gave her a faithful reproduction of the incident, plus something she had missed the first time around. She now saw it in a very different light, which was just as well, since she had indeed made a mistake the first time. The next day she received a birthday card from the colleagues whom she suspected so unjustly!

Another example of help given by a literal action-replay dream came from a man who dreamed he was driving his car along a familiar road and when he put his foot on the brake nothing happened and he crashed into a wall. He was not hurt but because it was such a realistic dream he felt sure it was a premonition of an impending accident. Interpreting this literally, I had to tell him that first and foremost it was a warning dream about the way he drove and the way he maintained his car, especially in relation to the brakes. He replied saying that his brakes badly needed relining but having done this he was now confident that the dream had been a warning after all, not a prophecy. To this I pointed out that it might well have been prophetic – if he had not heeded the warning it gave!

Our unconscious minds absorb much more than our conscious minds, and then take the trouble to project this information to us as literal dream warnings. True, under hypnosis similar details can sometimes be recalled, but with illuminating dreams like these, appearing at exactly the right time, who needs to bother with that?

SYMBOLIC DREAMS

Symbolic dreams arise from the unconscious mind and reflect our inner world of intuition and inspiration. This world is inhabited with feelings which for the most part cannot be expressed in words. Words like fear, anger, love and hate are merely superficial labels for these feelings; beyond this they cannot be intellectualized further. Experiencing them intuitively, however, is a very different matter. This is where dream symbology fits in, for this is to intuition what words are to intellect.

We are not as familiar with our inner world as we are with the outer, overshadowing world, mainly because right from childhood we are taught to keep a tight rein on feelings and suppress them altogether, if possible. When a child has a tantrum, this is regarded as something of a disgrace, yet how else can he express a particular feeling which the most intellectual adult could not put into words, let alone the child who cannot even speak? This is where symbolic dreams fit in. In the case of children, their frustrated feelings are freed in sleep and emerge as nightmares; their parents unknowingly contribute to the cause of these simply because they do not realize that both tantrums and dreams are wordless symbolic expressions.

Symbolic dreams, then, reflect feelings and emotions – but not all, by a long way, are concerned with hang-ups and bad experiences which cannot be put into words. Many give birth to intuition, inspirations, messages from God, the gods, an angel or some discarnate spirit. Psychic experiences and universal archetypes are expressed, too. The secret, however, of understanding messages from symbolic dreams is not to replace one symbol with another, as so often happens in psychic circles, for this only takes us further away, not closer, to the meaning. What we have to do is to bring it back into the realm of common sense and reasoning, otherwise it is impossible to ever understand its message.

Many symbolic dreams are metaphorical and should be interpreted as such. They should be understood in the same way as the saying 'Out of the frying pan and into the fire' – a word-picture warning that someone is going from one bad situation to another.

If we look at dream symbols in much the same way as we look at trademarks it is easy to understand the logic of the heart and the subtle force behind it. The commercial world of hard-sell advertising knows all about symbolism. Their advertising campaigns are based almost entirely on this principle, knowing that subliminal influence pays off handsomely, especially on the financial level! Our every-day outer world is injected with these clever symbolic innuendoes, with every advert appealing first to the heart, then to the head, and finally to the purse. Yet, as clever as these ploys are and as much petrol we buy because of the tiger it puts in the tank, our dreams are far, far cleverer than this.

It is the translating of dream symbols into reason that causes all the trouble, yet this is not difficult once the different worlds of the intuitive heart and the intellectual head have been recognized. True, they are as different as one of the five senses is from the others and we all know how hard it is to express one of these in terms of another. Try describing a sound in terms of the sense of smell. It is all a question of representational systems, each with its own set of rules and references, yet each is capable of expressing the same thing, differently.

The message from the following dream is an example of this and could easily have been dismissed as illogical ramblings if the dreamer had not been told that it represented an aspect of his own life. In that the dreamer was walking down an unfamiliar road when he reached a dark, miserable hovel. Grey clouds loomed overhead, and he went inside where he found a poor, pathetic creature wearing clothes similar to those his wife wore. He did not recognize this person and felt sorry for her.

In essence this is all there was to the dream, and on waking the misery and gloom weighed heavily on him all day. Having used a stand-in for his wife and substituted his familiar home with a dismal scene on the road to nowhere, his dreaming mind had done a good symbolic job on his existing domestic scene. The message from this, which came easily once it was applied to his own circumstances, showed all too clearly how dismal his homelife was and how he really did not know his own wife.

'PRACTICAL' DREAMS

Sometimes, the head and the heart, intelligence and intuition, do battle with the result that they 'blow a fuse' and produce a void not unlike the rapid transit system of those so-called black holes in space! Some might call this a brainstorm, a real nightmare, but whatever it is we still have to come down to earth and put such dream messages into action if we want to solve our problems. Problems are basically intellectual or psychological, but it does not follow that literal dreams necessarily represent practical problems and symbolic dreams represent psychological, heartfelt problems. Many tunes are being played at the same time!

Practical dreams, however, tend to reflect everyday problems associated with the home, work, career and all academic subjects. The realm of the head rules during the day mostly, but with a bit of luck the heart has its say at night, so again these dreams may be either symbolic, literal or a bit of both. One of the most profound examples of this was when Professor Kekule dreamed up the symbolic solution to his practical chemical problem, and so discovered the elusive benzine ring theory.

Less profoundly, one of my dreams helped me in a similar way. When first teaching relaxation I knew I needed a special piece of music to help with this, but gave up the search because none seemed to be what I was looking for. As soon as I stopped looking and listening outwardly, it was as if I gave my dreaming mind a chance: right away I dreamed of the music of a popular song, the name of which I never did find out. Instead of the usual quick tempo, though, it was played in the dream in a very slow four-four rhythm, rather in the style of the hymn 'O God our Help in Ages Past'. This did not mean anything at all to me until several weeks later when I read how research with music showed that the breathing rate, blood-pressure, heartbeat and brain waves all slowed down to keep in tune and in time with music that had four-four time, namely, 60 beats to the minute. This was the music I needed. It could be anything just so long as it was played slowly as a largo! Every time I hear that song now I want to hear it in that slow time, but the only time I ever did was in my dream.

PSYCHOLOGICAL DREAMS

Psychological dreams reflect inner personal problems like private thoughts, feelings, hopes, failures, fears, loves and all the secrets of the heart. These can be safely exposed in dreams without the fear of prying eyes and the passing of judgment from others. When crossed wires fuse and the memory filing system is disorganized, a psychological deram is then very useful in dredging up that which needs bringing to the surface. Often, the most helpful of these dreams are the nastiest, but when it is remembered that they are reflecting bad memories and poor situations anyway, this is exactly as they should be. Life is not a bed of roses, so why should dreams reflect anything other than the truth? This is just what this next dream did for a distressed woman.

In her dream she was in a wood, out-numbered by those who wanted to kill her. She felt she had to retaliate and kill them first, but when she was faced with the task of actually doing it she could not. This was because her assailants appeared to be pregnant, innocent-looking women who were not as fierce as they at first seemed. The uncomplicated interpretation of this dream shows a desire to commit psychological suicide because of being unable to face up to the situation symbolized by the dream. At the same time she knew for a fact that there were those who actually did wish her harm, probably as a result of something she had done, or not done, in the past. Retaliation, on her part, her dream showed, would be most unfair in the circumstances, but the good sign was the pregnant women – which meant that they, as well as the dreamer, would survive and come out of the wood with new hope for the future.

I later discovered that this dreamer's life was in a state of chaos following traumatic divorce proceedings where she was the so-called guilty party. By applying a bland interpretation to the circumstances only she knew, she was able to see her situation for what it was, and above all take comfort in the message that pregnant women symbolized a promise for the future. This, then, was a clarifying and sustaining dream which should have helped her to keep going until she was out of that particularly nasty wood!

When selecting psychological dreams to best illustrate their powers, it is difficult to choose any one as being more important than others since all are unique in their own way, but I suppose a dream that alters a person's life for the better, through him or her acting upon its message, is the one that matters most. Just such a dream came from a woman who wrote from a psychiatric ward where she had voluntarily placed herself. In the dream she found herself trapped in a cave, and although this did not frighten her unduly she knew she could not find her way out. Suddenly, a strange old woman appeared and quietly said, 'I can show you the way out.' After prodding with her stick, the old woman began making a hole in the rock until eventually it was big enough to allow the dreamer to escape into the daylight.

The message from this was so symbolically explicit it seemed a pity to desecrate it by putting it into harsh, inadequate words, but it had to be done if the dreamer was to accept and act consciously upon its message. Obviously, the cave represented the dreamer's unconscious mind, which had actually trapped her into believing it was safer to dwell in there than in the conscious outside world. It symbolized a sanctuary for her which she equated in reality with the security of the hospital ward. The old woman was the wise old woman within the dreamer, who had the power not only to get her out of her depression but liberate her from herself. The most important part of this message, however, was to show that she must and could rely on herself in the future, which is what she did and has done ever since the dream.

'And they dreamed a dream both of them, the butler and the baker of the King of Egypt, which were bound in prison. And Joseph saw them in the morning and they were sad and he asked "Whereof look you so sad today?" And they told him, "We dreamed a dream and there was no interpreter." And Joseph said to them, "Do not interpretations belong to God? Tell me them, I pray you." The butler told his dream to Joseph saying, "In my dream, behold, a vine was before me, with three branches, and it budded and blossom shot forth and the clusters brought forth ripe grapes. And Pharaoh's cup was in my hand and I took grapes and pressed them into his cup and gave it into Pharaoh's hand." "The three branches", said Joseph to the butler, "are three days; within three days Pharaoh will restore you to his service. And when he does,

make mention of me, Joseph, and bring me out of prison." When the baker heard the interpretation was good, he too asked Joseph for the meaning of his dream, also featuring the number three. "Behold," he said, "I had three white baskets on my head. In the uppermost one was baked bread and sweetmeats for Pharaoh and the birds did peck and eat this." And Joseph answered: "The three baskets are three days, yet within three days will Pharaoh hang thee on a tree and the birds shall eat thy flesh."' (Genesis 40:5–19.)

THE LANGUAGE OF DREAMS

When it comes to the langue of dreams, our dreaming mind does not limit itself in any way, extravagantly using all sorts of signs, symbols and words. Nor does it keep to one language, either, for the odd foreign phrase is often thrown in for good measure. But this is to be expected, because in so doing dreams are reflecting exactly what we do when awake anyway. We all talk a lot to get our message over and the conversation we use is made up of remarkable comparisons, puns and proverbs, so why should our dreams not follow suit? 'Out of the frying pan and into the fire' describes some situations perfectly, so imagine what scope this sort of talk gives to the dreaming mind when composing it into a dream. The transformation of a situation into a dream, incidentally, is very similar to that of a book being made into a film, but the unique thing about this is that the dreamer not only writes it, but is also screen director, stage manager, actor, actress and the viewing audience all rolled into one. If that is not pure magic, then I do not know what is!

SHAPES AND COLOURS

The basic language of dreams, as well as that of the unconscious, is one of shapes and colours. The first toys given to a baby, furry animals apart, are strange sets of coloured shapes. We see rows of bright beads strung across prams, and in cots lie assortments of red, yellow, green, blue and pink circles, triangles, squares, oblongs and ovals in various combinations and sizes. The baby did not choose them, but manufacturers – and adults whose unconscious minds know all about the basic language of the mind, although if you asked them, would deny all knowledge of it – did. In fact, grown-ups enjoy playing with these coloured shapes more than a baby, because this links them with that collective, fundamental world of shape and colour.

When a baby leaves the coloured shapes behind, they may be forgotten consciously but never unconsciously. Every single object they see in life from then on will be compared progressively with these colours and shapes, for these are their basic terms of reference for the outer world. Things, henceforth, will be described as round, square, triangular, oblong or oval, and although this simplicity is superceded by complicated and conventional objects and the distinct contrast in colours loses its brightness, the original shapes and colours are still retained in the memory. And for good reason.

When distinct coloured shapes appear in dreams, they often symbolize conditions relating to health. Just as there are over one hundred adjectives to describe pain, so too are there countless shapes to represent various complaints and conditions. In self-healing techniques using conscious imagery and visualization, every symptom, fear or pain is transformed into a basic abstract in the form of a coloured shape. Having done this, the mind is then in a position to control the condition and reverse the negative, destructive psychosomatic force into a positive, creative one, and so bring about healing. Although as self-healing this is a consciously controlled exercise, our dreaming mind often does this spontaneously, and it can be requested to do so by incubation.

As well as representing physical and mental conditions, shapes and colours also convey principles, energies and moods. Red, for example, always symbolizes physical energy, like hard work, energy-drive and sex. Sometimes it reflects anger, as in the case of 'a red rag to a bull'. Violet, on the other hand, symbolizes spiritual things. Green, the colour in the middle of the light spectrum represents emotions. The meaning and association of these colours is traditionally inherited from the collective unconscious and they apply not only in dream symbolism but to everything else in life generally. Green, for example, has instinctively been recognized and used as an emotionally stabilizing colour, hence hospital wards and classrooms were once decorated throughout in this colour.

PREMONITION DREAMS

The majority of dreams are by no means profound truths or startling prophecies, although all have their message and meaning. Life is full of trivia posing trivial problems, so it is to be expected that our dreams trade heavily in these too. Shopping, walking, office filing and the many other routine and boring tasks can all be reassessed and reflected in dreams, but for the most part the really insignificant ones are soon forgotten. Dreams reflect the person and his lifestyle, so if we lead boring lives then we have boring dreams, or remember none of them because there is not much to remember. If, on the other hand, our lives are full of ambition, enthusiasm and creativity, then our dreams will likewise mirror all this and more. Even so, run-of-the-mill dreams still bring minor warnings and can be insignificantly prophetic, showing, if nothing else, that the context of a dream is very different from and has nothing whatsoever to do with the type of dream.

When premonitions are mentioned, one immediately thinks of some world-shattering event having been foreseen in a dream. Several people dreamed of the sinking of the Titanic, the coming of the Second World War and political assassinations, but what is not realized is that the majority of premonitions are as trivial as the time they foresaw that the milkman would leave only two pints of milk next Wednesday instead of three. These insignificant yet still prophetic dreams are far more common than most realize. How often the odd word said during the day invokes the memory of the previous night's dream.

Although prophetic dreams can help in a dozen or more different ways, including preparing us for the imminent death of relatives or even mere acquaintances, many still appear to serve no useful purpose whatsoever. Maybe we have to wait a long while before their significance is recognized, by which time we will probably have forgotten them. It was just such a dream I had in 1963 that decided for me that dreams were meant to play an important part in my life, although its prophetic content could not in any way alter events that later came true. All it did was to prove to me, quite conclusively, that there were definitely such things as prophetic dreams.

Following a tour of American hospitals with a group of British radiographers, I managed to sandwich in a very brief meeting with an aunt who lived in St Louis, but I did not go to her home, she came to see me in Minneapolis. About six weeks after returning home I had a spectacular dream showing this aunt pacing up and down her backyard, as she called it, in a furious distraught state. She told me clearly in this dream that the cause of her anger was a man called Grayson. This so impressed me that I wrote to her at once asking if anything was wrong and if she knew of anyone called Grayson. She soon replied saying she was fine and that she had never heard of anyone called Grayson, so I forgot all about it until, that is, she came to London two years later. On meeting her, she immediately thrust my letter about the dream into my hand. What had happened was that one year after she received it she found herself in a terrible rage, pacing up and down her back-yard. Apparently, a new boss had taken over where her husband worked and sacked all the older men, which understandably made my aunt extremely angry. To let off steam she went out into her backyard, where here her memory must have rung some sort of bell because she suddenly remembered my letter, which she had kept. Reading it over she was staggered to discover the name Grayson. This was the name of her husband's new boss!

At the time I had this dream, the man in question was totally unknown not only to me and my aunt but to her husband as well, so this completely rules out tele-pathic communication as a possible explanation.

Premonitions seem to result from extrasensory percep-tion, with no apparent conscious or unconscious link with the past, present, or future, and predict events which no living person could possibly have deduced logically beforehand. Even inspired guesses can be ruled out, as

well as subliminal perception, because the true premoni-
tion gives names and places and sometimes dates of
future events. It is acausal; there is no chain of action
and reaction.

Psychic or Incubus Attacks

One example of thought transference in dreams, however, is when we pick up stray thoughts that are negative
or, even worse, receive those aimed specifically at us,
against our will. These cause terrible nightmares known
as psychic or incubus attacks. Children are especially
vulnerable to these. Usually, terrifying black shapes,
shadows and creepie-crawlie things are described as
insinuating their way into their dreams. An incubus, by
definition, is an evil spirit that descends on those asleep
and attempts to possess or take over and influence the
dreamer's thoughts. This definition covers a multitude of
sins, of course, from impressions received from malevo-
lent ghosts to the reception of strong, dominant thoughts

specifically projected to the dreamer from a person who wishes them harm.

These attacks have been recognized for centuries and there have always been ways said to protect against them. The Victorians favoured prayers picked out in needlework cross-stitch, which they hung above their beds, whilst others preferred a picture of Jesus on the wall and a crucifix under their pillow. As external symbols of divine power, these help tremendously, but are only secondary compared with taking responsibility for our own protection. After all, if we take the trouble to protect ourselves at night from intruders on a practical level by bolting doors and windows, why not on a psychic and mental level too?

PSYCHIC PROTECTION

As a guard against these attacks, there is a simple and effective mental ritual that keeps out unwanted influences and stimuli, including bad telepathic thoughts from others. This protection depends on the energy field surrounding us, composed of heat, sound and electrical impulses, plus a subtler force field usually referred to as the aura. It is a blend of these that protects us, but if we are tired, rundown, ill or depressed, this barrier becomes drained and is insufficient to keep all at bay. The aim, therefore, of this exercise is to build up this positive energy field.

This should be carried out just before going to sleep. Having settled down warmly in bed, lie flat on your back, close your eyes and breathe in to the count of two, and out to the count of three or even four, thus imitating the sleep breathing rhythm. To relax physically, turn your attention to both feet and clench up the toes for a second or two and then relax them. Next, move both ankles a little and turn up your toes towards your head and then let them go. Think of your knees and thighs as resting. Now turn your attention to your hands: clench your fists and then relax them. Concentrate next on your spine as it relaxes, and your shoulders too. Feel the gravitational forces anchoring you to the bed, holding you there like a magnet. Think now of your face and know that all the lines and furrows have gone and your face is smooth.

You will now be relaxed and ready to carry out a simple self-protection ritual. In your mind's eye, see an energy field around you. See it as a blue, white or gold light that completely envelops you as a protective cloak, and know that inside it you are utterly safe. Nothing can penetrate this barrier. It is as simple as that, so please try it if ever the need arises.

Children who have recurring nightmares, where the same frightening entity scares them night after night, are helped if given some coloured crayons and paper and asked to draw the nasty apparition that scares them so. When they have done this – which I might add is usually drawn in grey or black – tell them that these things love the dark, so right over the original drawing get the child to draw a big, strong, yellow sun, sending its rays of light into all the dark corners. This reduces fear tremendously, and by introducing it as a game, the child's confidence grows and with it their positivity and natural protection. On a purely practical level, though, if a light is kept on, even a small one, it is found that many such nightmares are prevented, anyway!

HEALING THOUGHTS

Thoughts are projections of energy and, like all forms of energy, can be used for good or bad, depending on their origin and intention. Negative thoughts in the form of external stimuli produce nightmares and psychic attacks, but the complete reverse of this is possible, too. When we are asleep we are far more receptive to external stimuli, for the simple reason that we are less aware of our five physical senses which flood our minds when awake. We might as well, therefore, make use of the positive forces, which are there as well as the negative.

Healing is given in our dreams in a variety of ways. Some produce practical solutions which, when tried work wonders, so as sources of solace we can be sure that dreams are there waiting to be of service to us. Sometimes it seems to be more of a waking experience than a dream, where the spirit of a doctor who died years ago appears at a patient's bedside and dispenses healing potions. On waking there is always much improvement in the patient's condition, which they link directly with the help brought to them in the night by the strange spectre. Many hospitals, not surprisingly, are said to have their healing ghosts. The most famous is the Grey Lady at St Thomas's Hospital in London, who has been seen by nurses and a former matron as well as by many patients. This ghost ministers to sleeping patients through their dreams who, on waking, find themselves well on the road to recovery.

GUILT DREAMS

No one ever dreams of having sex with one's regular bed partner if sex is there for the asking, because there is no need. On the other hand, when it is not there we have to concede that Freud was right with his wish-fulfilment and sublimation interpretations. Having sex in public places is by no means rare in dreams, and it shows quite clearly that the dreamer is suffering from some form of guilt complex, but not necessarily sexual.

A recent dream I interpreted led me to believe that the sex the dreamer had in a supermarket amid the canned soups was more an act of diversion. What with helping herself and being 'in the soup', shoplifting was symbolically implied far more than anything else

Just as Freud thought ordinary objects were disguised sex symbols, I have found that sex, as a symbol in its own right, stands for ordinary – or rather, extraordinary –

activities far removed from love-making. Apart from shoplifting, sex in dreams represents dominance in business. I have also found it represents jealousy and one-upmanship generally.

If we decide a sex dream is mainly literal, then the message probably applies to our sex lives and our outlook on this subject. Symbolically, snakes are a favourite sex symbol but, in fact, they represent energy drives generally, and since sex is only one of those drives, the context in which the snake appears gives the clue to the level of energy it represents. They can, therefore, indicate ambitions, temptations, hidden powers, secret activities, forces of nature and healing ability, or down-to-earth deviousness like the proverbial snake in the grass.

RECURRING DREAMS

The dream that recurs time and time again does so simply because its message has not been received and understood. Once it is, it stops immediately, for its work is done.

Some dreamers have experienced the same dream, on and off, since childhood, with the same old record being played time and time again. Others, however, experience them over shorter periods, with repeats covering only a few weeks or months. One woman had a recurring nightmare from earliest childhood in which she was always alone in a deep pit. From behind a rock a lion would suddenly appear and spring at her, at which point she would wake up screaming! It was not until she was quite old, and still having virtually the same nightmare at two- to three-monthly intervals, that I explained the possibility that these could be action-replays from a previous life, where she had, in fact, been thrown to the lions. At first she rejected this as outright nonsense because she did not believe in reincarnation. As time went by, however, she warmed to the idea and finally accepted that it might just be possible. From then on the nightmares ceased.

In no way does this prove reincarnation, but what it does prove is that the explanation was sufficient to put

an end to a deep-seated fear. To know the devil is to overcome it, and there is more than one devil! Hypnosis,
once believed to be infallible and reveal only truthful
past events, has been proved to substitute explanations
for phobias and fears, so if reasonable they can replace
the original misnomer and all will be well. The mistaken
association of ideas, with memories filed in the wrong
place, is the usual explanation. In fact, the woman with
the bad lion dream may have been re-enacting a tale
told to her at far too young an age! Either way, the ghost
of the fearful lion was laid.

SCHEMING DREAMS

It is often asked why dreams are so scheming, devious
and complicated. The answer is that they are not. There
is nothing in them that we have not put there ourselves,
even though some may have been triggered by external
stimuli. Dreams reveal, they do not conceal. The com-
plexities of life today are such that we do not have

enough time to solve our problems before going to sleep, so consequently much of our dream-time is taken up with action-replays and symbolically reflected dreams showing mixed-up situations. Although dreams are well able to help us out in this way, if we leave too much for them to sort out it does not give our dreaming mind time to pass on those original messages that have the power to inspire and motivate the genius within. The mere fact of realizing that this is possible is often all that is needed to alter a life-long pattern of dreaming, and when this happens we are then ready to truly learn to dream!

'The question was put to him, what is hope? And his answer was the dream of waking man.' – Diogenes

CHAPTER FOUR

UNDERSTANDING OUR DREAMS: A DREAM DIARY

Before we can interpret dreams, we must first have material on which to work, so for this we need to keep a dream diary. It was Edgar Casey's son Hugh Lyn who said that the best book we shall ever read on dreams is the one we write ourselves. He was, of course, referring to our personal dream diary. Many people conscientiously keep a most orderly account of their boring daytime happenings, yet never consider recording their nightlife which, if they did but know it, is far more instructive, interesting and exciting!

THE DREAM DIARY

There are no hard-and-fast rules relating to dreams, even when it comes to keeping a record of them, but it helps to have a few practical guidelines.

RULE 1: THE DIARY

The first rule in keeping a dream diary is very practical indeed, but at the same time ritualistic. It is this. Go out and buy an attractive notebook and pen expressly for this purpose. This is the first commitment, too, and as an act of faith it alerts the dreaming mind to the fact that we really mean business. Once having bought these, place them by your bed, where they must at all costs stay, because if they wander we cannot possibly afford to hunt for them in the middle of the night when they are most needed. We might find them, but at the expense of losing a valuable dream.

RULE 2: THE NUMBER, THE DATE AND THE TIME

The second rule concerns the numbering, dating and if possible noting the time of each dream. It is important that the day and the date are clearly written at the top of a fresh page each night in readiness. The merit in this will become more and more apparent as we continue to do so, for it is only in retrospect that some warnings can be seen and prophecies recognized. Dating also reveals sequences and series of dreams, and recurring dreams plus many other surprising features, not least being the revelation that the dreaming mind is a fantastic calendar and clock. Forgotten birthdays, anniversaries and events that happened long ago on a certain date are remembered, and even events that are to happen in the future may be indicated, too. Numbering dreams in the order of appearance is also important. Some nights there will be more than one to record, so continue with the numerical sequence. If the time of the dream is known – or rather the waking time coinciding with it – this should be recorded too.

RULE 3: SPEED

The third rule is that we must write down all we can remember about a dream or dreams immediately on waking, and this means before we have thought of or done anything else whatsoever. Dreams fade very quickly and many can be captured only by putting them down on paper at once. This fading of dreams is another reason why so many people vow they never dream, but they would be amazed to discover they did, if they followed the simple but vital rule of putting pen to paper instantly they opened their eyes! If, however, a dream does initially evade us it nevertheless leaves an impression behind in the form of a particular mood, feeling or atmosphere, so note this.

Rule 4: Filling-in

The fourth rule is to fill in all the gaps. It takes considerable willpower to snatch up a pen at 2 in the morning, but believe it or not this soon becomes an exciting habit. It also serves to keep our dreaming mind informed that we still mean serious business. Hopefully, most dream recording can be done first thing in the morning, but whatever the time, never mind the scribble. This can be sorted out later in the harsh light of day. The vital thing is to record as much as we can remember, as fast as possible.

When we have done all this, we are then in possession of a good rough sketch, but this needs going over, there and then, for missed details. A time delay at this stage robs us of valuable evidence, so on this second time around look for any colours that stand out, remembering that colours fade first and faster than other parts of the dream, hence the belief that some dreams are in black and white. Look, too, for conversation pieces, words, songs or poems – everything that comes to mind. Having added this we now write down anything that reminds us of an event from the previous day, such as a TV programme, a conversation, an incident, a worry, or a problem we have on our mind. These associations are priceless when it comes to the interpretation.

RED

Physical energy: an improvement in health; antagonism – the proverbial red rag to a bull.

ORANGE

A friendly colour associated with social activity and cheerfulness. Depending on the circumstances this colour is either telling you to cheer up, or pointing out that you need to.

YELLOW

The colour of the sunshine, relating to intellectual matters. it is a clear colour, so seeing this in your dream tells you to think with your head – your intellect – to solve a problem.

GREEN

Peace and relaxation. You either need more of this or you can expect it in the future, if this colour predominates.

BLUE

The colour for protection. This ties in with the blue sky which protects the earth from harmful radiation. Seeing blue in a dream may, therefore, indicate that you need to protect yourself in some way or, conversely, you are feeling 'blue'.

INDIGO

Intuitive and instinctive qualities so this colour encourages you to allow your heart, the seat of inner feeling, to rule for a while.

VIOLET

The colour nearest to heaven, symbolizes spiritual aspirations and religious beliefs.

Finally, make a list of all signs and symbols. These will be in the form of people, animals, monsters, figures, objects, shapes and universal archetypes including religious and mysterious symbols.

At an appropriate moment during the next day, the night's dream has to be tidied up, probably re-written and put in some order in readiness for interpretation. Scrap paper, incidentally, can be used for that first rough draft, and then the final version can be written neatly into the dream diary later. This means that scrap paper has to be at the ready, but it is well worth the extra effort especially if we have to write in the dark, which is often the case if we do not want to disturb someone else!

The important features entered in a dream diary will, therefore, include the following, in this order: The number, date and time of the dream. *The Dream itself.* The atmosphere, feeling or mood and any colours it left behind. Special conversation pieces, words, songs or poems. A list of signs and symbols. Previous associations. The finished product of a night's dreaming could look something like the page from my dream diary, for the night of 17 March 1983, showing two very different dreams. Incidentally, if we think daytime diaries are revealing, they are nothing compared with their night-time counterparts waiting to emerge!

- *Date:* Thursday 17 March 1983
- *Dream Number:* 40

- *Time:* Don't know but before 6 a.m.
- *The Dream:* I was trying to do up a necklace but had great difficulty in doing so. A voice said quite distinctly 'Try, try, try again.'
- *Atmosphere:* Ordinary.
- *Mood:* Alert.
- *Signs and Symbols:* Necklace.
- *Words:* Try, try, try again.
- *Previous Associations:* Seen bank statements yesterday and wondered how to make ends meet.

- *Dream Number:* 41
- *Time:* Between 6 a.m. and 8 a.m.
- *The Dream:* I was walking with someone on a hill and saw a large brown friendly snake rolling happily down the hillside. We walked down and when we reached more level ground I noticed some really bright yellow flowering shrubs and some almost unnaturally mauve flowers. In the dream I recognized

them as Laburnum and an early flowering shrub called Daphne. I was also aware that it was a dream so I decided there and then to answer some of the questions asked by Dr Keith Herne in his question-naire on lucid dreaming. One of these I knew was 'Are the colours in your dream (a) brighter than in real life (b) the same as in real life (c) less bright than in real life? I decided they were exactly the same. I then wanted to show the person I was with the snake but could not find it.

- *Atmosphere:* Nice, bright and sunny.
- *Mood:* Happy and inquisitive.
- *Signs and Symbols:* A person, a friend. A hillside and level ground, unrecognized. A large brown friendly snake. Brightly coloured flowers.
- *Words:* None spoken but plenty of thoughts.
- *Names:* Daphne and Dr Keith Herne.
- *Previous Associations:* Dr Herne's project.

THE INCUBATION OF DREAMS

By keeping a dream diary it soon became clear that the majority of our dreams are concerned with practical matters and psychological relationships, and only rarely do they spontaneously come to our aid to solve a specific problem. The ancient races recognized dreams as great sources of enlightenment and so took steps to link individual minds with God and lesser divinities whom they looked upon as His messengers. By attuning themselves to one of these deities they requested a dream that would help them with their problems. This form of dream incubation was appropriate to that bygone age but today there are no shrines dedicated to Morpheus nor are there oracular priests who will assist us to dream to order. This, however, does not mean that the age of dream miracles is past. Far from it, but we live in a different age now, one where we must make our own contacts and incubate our own dreams.

The powers that be have certainly not deserted us, although we may have deserted them. The gods and goddesses, angels and God's messengers are still very much with us, if we look, for they are those forces Jung called the universal archetypes. Nor are we without oracles; our own dreaming mind is exactly this. By tuning in to ourselves, we can therefore request and receive answers and help just as surely as our ancestors once did.

Dreaming is an art and, like most arts, it needs practice. True, we all dream and often receive help from dreams at the right time, but this is more by luck than judgment compared with what can be achieved if we put ourselves out. Since most of us are content to leave it all to our dreaming mind, what more should we expect than the usual run-of-the-mill dreams concerned with everyday matters and only the occasional fantastic experiences? If, however, we consciously co-operate with our dreaming mind, it is so pleased to be recognized that it becomes our obedient servant overnight!

Just as no one else can digest our food for us, nor can they solve our problems. Our life is always our own responsibility. With dreams we are working entirely with ourselves thus making it an excellent exercise in self-reliance, and since dreams are messages from ourselves to ourselves, this makes a lot of sense.

It has often been said that God helps those who help themselves and this was never truer than when applied to the incubation of dreams. The untapped potential of our mental resources is more than enough to keep us safe and secure, not to mention healthy and wise, but who can wonder that we receive so little help from this source when we barely recognize its existence, let alone its power. Through our dreams all is possible.

The incubation of dreams simply means asking our dreaming mind for help, but even in this day and age when we are both oracle and dreamer, we still need a mental ritual to co-ordinate ourselves with archetypal forces. Each of us, however, must go about this in the way that suits us best. If we feel we would rather rely entirely on God, then the request for a special dream should be made in the form of an invocative prayer. All religions tell us that God speaks to us through our dreams, so there is no reason why we should not ask for His help in this way. On the other hand, by appealing to our innermost selves, that part of us some call the soul or spirit, we can receive equally good results. Maybe the answers and stimuli come from the same divine source – who knows – we are all part of the Creation, after all.

Joan of Arc's dreams convinced her that she was to be the saviour of France. From these, she contrived original schemes which persuaded the Dauphin that she was indeed capable of such victories. In G. B. Shaw's play St Joan, *she is accused of listening to imaginary voices in her dreams. To this she replies: 'Of course, that is how messages of God do come.' For proof of this she could have referred her interrogators to the biblical text found in Job 33:14–16 which says: 'For God speaketh once, yea twice, yet man perceiveth it not. In a dream, in a vision of the night when deep sleep falleth upon slumbering men upon their bed, then He openeth their ears and sealeth in their instructions.'*

HEAD AND HEART AGAIN

The time to incubate dreams is when we are in bed, warm, relaxed and ready to go to sleep. The difficulty, though, is relaxing in the first place. It helps, I find, if we say, 'I can't solve it intelligently with my head when awake, so over to you, dreaming mind.' This works well, for it off-loads or shifts responsibility from one part of us to another which is better equipped to take the burden. Having carried out this silent verbal ritual, we then need to relax physically, with the exercise on page 107.

Now is the time to begin the incubation of a dream. We must contact that part of us which is responsible for sending us dreams and speak to it silently but positively, like this: 'Please, dreaming mind, send me a dream that will help me.' Into this request we incorporate pleas like 'please give me a sign; please direct energy to that part of me that needs healing: tell me how I can best help those who ask for my help, or what shall I do?' Each plea will be different, of course, but the sharper and more concise we can make it, the more cut and dried will be the response. Having made our request in the most concise way possible, we now tell ourselves that we are ready and waiting to receive a message and that we are going to write down all we can remember about the dream immediately on waking.

How we incubate our dreams is up to us entirely with much depending on our way of life and our religious beliefs, but probably a different approach for different situations is best. Finally, when a special dream has been received we must always remember to thank God, the powers that be and ourselves, for sending it to us.

The Interpretation of Dreams

The best person to interpret dreams is none other than the dreamer himself. After all, he alone constructed them using props from his own private store of memories, experiences and associations. This, however, is not to say that someone else cannot interpret them for us at face value because they can. But this is only half the story. Having been given a message, it is then up to the dreamer to apply this to his own personal set of circumstances, which he alone knows. Then, and only then, will the interpretation be complete and of any real value.

The more dreams we investigate, our own and others, the more we learn to understand them, but there is one trap into which we must not fall: when interpreting dreams for others, we must not impose upon them our own association of ideas. We have built these up from unique, personal experiences, and they apply only to our own dreams, not other people's. As dream analysts we are able to recognize the literal and symbolic content, see puns and double meanings, translate signs and symbols, all of which give us an overall message, but this is still meaningless to everyone else except the dreamer. It is up to them to link this face-value meaning with secret inner knowledge, in order to bring about that alchemical fusion between the dream and reality.

To interpret dreams, two qualifications are necessary. One is that we must have a true desire to do so and the other is that we have enough enthusiasm to sustain that desire. To remember and analyse the odd dream here and there is one thing, but really to get to grips with them is quite another matter. To do this we have to make a personal commitment, but this is most rewarding for we soon learn so much more about ourselves, our pecking order in society and even our place in the universe. If 'Know Thyself' means anything at all, then there is no better way to seeking this than through our own dreams.

Having started a personal dream diary, we will soon be in possession of at least one well-recorded dream, remembering that whichever type of dream it is, from the mundane to the esoteric, the same basic principles of interpretation will apply. In some dreams it will be the atmosphere that is all important, whilst in others it will be the dialogue that stands out. Each dream, however, will be uniquely different and this, along with its other dominant qualities, is what we need to discover for ourselves.

THE FEEL OF A DREAM

Feelings speak louder than words; they are also difficult to put into words, so the first step towards interpreting a dream is to discover its feeling, mood or atmosphere. This can be seen as the backcloth on the stage of dreams before which all else is arranged. Props are set up, actors and actresses appear and the action takes place. Sometimes the feeling is all that is left, and although getting out of bed on the 'wrong' side in the morning is often blamed for a dark mood shadowing us all day, this is really due to a 'hangover' from a forgotten dream. This left-over mood is not always negative; it can be positive, extremely cheerful and full of confidence, in which case we feel great and happy that the cloud from yesterday has lifted. This is because we have slept on it, as the saying goes, and although the details of the night's dreaming were not consciously remembered, the sum total of their workings-out, in the shape of a feeling, were. In this we can see the power our dreams have in colouring the next day in our life, if not our entire future.

The feel of a dream is a message in itself. The setting under the midday sun can only evoke a scene of hope and sunnier days for the future but, on the other hand, what an abject picture of misery the gloomy half-light paints of heavy depression. The atmosphere is accurately reflected in colours and shades of light and dark. Look closely, therefore, at feelings, moods and atmospheres, which includes weather conditions, in your dreams before all else. If these are missed it can mean that the whole interpretation is based on a false premise or, worse, none at all.

THE ARTIST WITHIN

The next task is to decide how much of a dream is literal, and how much is symbolic. If we visit an art gallery we see three types of paintings – literal, symbolic, and those which are a mixture of both. The comparison between these and dreams is striking, so it helps to think about a dream as a painting before considering characters, action and dialogue.

The literal painting depicts a true-to-life scene as clearly as any photograph. Like its literal dream coun-terpart, nothing is left to the imagination. Shops are shops, houses are houses, people are themselves and trees are trees, right down to the last twig. The message may lie in the importance of the details we miss and take for granted as we rush blindly by.

At first glance the symbolic or abstract painting, like its comparative dream, looks a right mess, almost meaningless to all who pass by except, that is, to the artist. Splashes of violent colours racing across the canvas produce a riot of shapes and shadows, and all attempts to see it as a conventional picture fail hopelessly. As we look more closely, we may come to sense that the angry red splashes are yesterday's rage, the dark shadows are today's threats, and the gold and white lines are rays of hope for the future. We now see and feel a symbolic cry, not from the head but from the heart.

The third painting – and many dreams are like this – is a literal and symbolic mixture. It depicts a recognizable though monstrous symbolic female with eyes at the back of her head and an ear to the ground. This artist has blended fact with fiction cleverly to represent his own biased, personal view of someone or something in his life. We can see, once we know what to look for, how his mind grabbed at the outer world for obvious signs and then dived down into secret inner recesses in search of a few symbols in order to concoct this literal and symbolic caricature.

The dreaming mind is definitely the artist within. The difference, though, between the dream artist and the other artist is that the inner artist has unlimited talent. Using colours in ways the Renoirs, Turners and Michelangelos of this world only dreamed about, the dream artist produces brown studies and blood moods as easily as he or she floods the canvas of the mind with colours from an ethereal rainbow. From the archetypal mystical heights to the abysmal depths, its power to create is unbelievable.

Although every dream is unique there are certain actions, objects, people and scenes which make regular appearances in dreams. These are the collective symbols and, although they have the same overall meaning, their messages are different when applied to individual circumstances. For example, we all experience similar problems in life – domestic worries, difficulties with relationships, loss of an aim, frustrated ambition, etc., so it is not surprising that these are represented by similar imagery.

SIGNS AND SYMBOLS

Signs and symbols are tackled next. These are recognized as people, animals, objects and designs, ranging from an ordinary kitchen mug to an esoteric version of the Holy Grail. There is, however, no definite dividing line between a sign and a symbol, because they merge and stand in for each other constantly.

Generally signs are literal images recognizable as people, animals and real objects, but even so this does not mean they necessarily have to be taken at face value! More often than not they represent someone or something else, so unless we recognize, say, a horse as the literal sign of a horse in an action-replay dream, it is masquerading as energy in the form of drive and horse-power. Just as a latchkey, unless relating to one lost recently, indicates a clue to a situation or the opening of a door on new opportunities. A ladder, a steamroller, a hammer and a thousand and one other objects are all frequently used by our dreaming mind in much the same way, so we must be prepared to recognize them metaphorically and not necessary literally.

Symbols represent principles and ideas, and they always stand for something more than their face value. Sometimes they appear as abstract shapes, mystical designs and religious insignia, but mainly they are recognizable signs used as stand-ins. For example, when a horse is used to represent energy, or a key a clue, they change from signs into symbols. There is little mystery in dream symbology in this respect, since most of it comes not from the collective unconscious but from the outer worldly environment flooded with metaphorical words and phrases like 'high horsepower', the 'lion's share', and 'barged into', not to mention the more personal descriptions like 'fiery temper', 'icy manner', 'snake in the grass' and 'silly ass'. Some of these signs-turned-symbols – such as snakes, for example – were used in this way long before man could read and write, so are now traditional symbols bordering on the archetypal. This is where a dictionary helps, but most words describing literal images with double meanings need only a little imagination plus personal associations to reveal their hidden message. Take the dream where the dominant sign is a bulldozer. Who could fail to miss the metaphorical implication that someone is about to be forced into uncompromising submission?

Only when a dream is literal can people, animals and objects be interpreted as themselves. Whilst it is not too difficult to see objects and even animals symbolically, it is not easy to see a person as being anything other than themselves, especially if they are close to us. Or is it? After all, we are all something to someone else. We are a son or a daughter for a start. Once we take the impersonal viewpoint, which is what the dreaming mind does, we can soon see the game it is playing. People cease to be themselves. They are still recognizable people, but as mother, father, daughter, son, grandparent, or friend they represent not personal individuals, but the impersonal image of the character. Add to this first names, all of which have their own meanings, and pet names like chick, ducks and kitten, and the circle of impressions widens even more!

Extending this one step further, we can see why the dreaming mind has little difficulty in finding candidates for projecting the message of idiot, fool or louse!

PARENT FIGURES AND FAMILY

Parents and grandparents often put in an appearance in our dreams. As strong as the temptation is to interpret them as themselves, nine times out of ten they are representing principles of an image. Our mothers in a symbolic context represent not themselves but feminine principles of comfort, compassion and sometimes the overbearing powers of the Great Mother earth, whilst our fathers represent the masculine dominance of authority and even the Father image of God Himself. Similarly, a brother or sister represents brotherly or sisterly platonic love.

One step removed from family images is the faceless status symbol. The dustman, the doctor, the typist, the plumber, the nurse and the lawyer, all literally recognized, have their symbolic counterpart, so when a policeman turns up in a dream we can bet law and order in our lives are involved.

To sum up, then, literal dreams reflecting the outer world use signs like people who play themselves and objects which can be taken at face value. Symbolic dreams, reflecting inner thoughts, use literal stand-ins with symbol meanings as well as using purely abstract symbols which include mythological creatures, mazes and universal archetypes. Whatever the sign or symbol, it always plays a unique role in each dream, but at the same time some are used repeatedly to convey, in essence, the same basic meaning. Apart from members of the family being used in this way, so too are houses, water, explosions, animals, trees and cars, trains, boats, aeroplanes, buses and bikes.

Written into every dream is a message, but in addition to this, advice and solutions are often given. Apart from literal messages which we can take at face value, there are those with their messages just below the surface. To discover these we have to follow the clues in a practical way and, as with the association of ideas, arrive at surprising but applicable conclusions and even remedies.

CONVERSATION, WORDS AND DIALOGUE

Often it is not what we say but the way we say it that makes the most impact, so if there is any dialogue in a dream note the intonation first. 'This is a fine state of affairs' may in fact be describing the complete opposite from what has been said. The dreaming mind knows all about this sort of double talk. Words are signs and symbols in themselves, so if we cannot take them at face value, we have to interpret them metaphorically. Sometimes, though, the message is to be taken literally but the situation is symbolic. One instance of this was the dream I had about trying to do up a necklace. The message of 'Try, try, try again' was to be taken literally, whereas the fastening of the necklace was symbolic, representing the situation.

PUNS AND RIDDLES

The dreaming mind produces puns and riddles every bit as good as those found in Christmas crackers, assuring us that we have incredible literary abilities when asleep, if not when awake! Pet names have great punning potential, as do body parts.

Expressions, such as 'handing over', 'head in that direction', 'get it off your chest', 'let's get to the bottom of things' and 'I can't stand it' are just a few examples of this type. Then there are parable puns like 'putting your foot in it', 'get your oar in there', 'face the music' and 'pie in the sky', all of which are easily missed unless we keep our ear to the ground!

Finally, there are some common-or-garden verbal puns where the names are the same but the spelling is sometimes different. Horse and hoarse, guilt and gilt, shoo and shoe, red and read, sole and soul and heel and heal are a few examples. One way of exposing these and other puns generally is to read the dream out loud – but on the quiet, of course!

Previous Associations

If a previous association is noted in the dream diary, then this is the next aspect to be taken into account. Late-night television is notorious for making its way into dreams but this is not the cause nor the stimulus that triggered it off. Whilst viewing the screen the dreaming mind, like a good journalist, is always on the look-out for original material to incorporate into a dream setting. If, for example, there is a lively skirmish this would serve as a wonderful battleground for a fight between the dreamer and some person or problem he or she is wrestling with!

Social gatherings are rich sources too, as the man who spent the previous evening in a busy pub, exclusively in male company, found out. His subsequent dream was an action-replay of the pub scene but with one big difference. His friends were not all male, but all female!

THE DREAM PLAY

A dream is usually a series of events, similar to a play. There are those with many acts and scenes, and those centred around one central happening. The main difference is that in dream plays, the dreamer decides on the title, theme and action, writes all the script, puts in the puns, innuendoes and double talk, designs the scenery, arranges the props, casts the actors and actresses and then promptly goes and sits in the front row of the audience to watch.

Having created these characters, it also follows that the dreamer plays them as well, putting words into their mouths that he would like to hear. If, however, the dreaming mind is impartial, which it can be, then these characters will be portrayed in a much more realistic and not so emotional way.

If, when we read a dream through to look for puns, we look at it as if it were a play, the action and any dialogue will reveal the role each person is playing, and with it the overall dream theme. Themes help to give a title to a dream as well as putting what it is saying into a nutshell. All dreams have individual themes and, however long or short the dream, its theme should be expressed as simply and concisely as possible. Even a rambling saga beginning on a cliff top, long-windedly describing the descent of the dreamer to the beach where he watches a tidal wave approach and race towards the shore, inundating and drowning many people, followed by the eventual escape of the dreamer up the cliff to safety, can be summed up in the explicit sentence: 'A threatening situation will or can be overcome.'

THE MESSAGE AND THE SOLUTION

Hopefully, all the effort put into unravelling a dream, which includes discovering its backcloths, props, people, signs and symbols, will unite and transform into a coherent message. Like dreams themselves, though, some messages will be short and simple whilst others will be long and less concise.

When a message reveals a difficult situation, as it so often does, a solution or way out is usually to be found in the dream too, and this can be even more important than the message, although it is, of course, really part of it.

Just as a warning dream will remain a warning dream and not end up prophetic if the message is acted upon, so the reverse is true of dreams revealing a problem with a potential solution. The key, in both instances, is to act upon the message, thus preventing or facilitating that which is possible.

A PRACTICAL GUIDE
TO THE INTERPRETATION

Having noted all the information given in our dream diary, we are now ready to begin on the interpretation. The practical aspect to be noted first is the date of the dream. This may or may not match up with an anniversary. Next, we try to re-create the mood the dream left behind, and remember the atmosphere in which it all took place. This will reveal degrees of warning or the reverse, boosts of encouragement and hope for the future. By looking at the dream as if it were a painting, it will then be fairly obvious if it is predominantly literal or symbolic. Either way, it must first be assumed to have a literal message.

When interpreting your dreams you must learn your own inner dream language, which is a combination of collective symbolism and your own.

Only when this refuses to fit into the picture should a symbolic or mystical meaning be even considered. Those people who see all their dreams as great mystical truths often spend their lives, literally, in their dreams and never put whatever those great truths are into practice. This is not to say that their interpretations are wrong, but by not associating and anchoring them to their practical everyday life they remain as so much pie-in-the-sky and, as such, are wasted. We must make use of our dreams down here, not marvel at them, up there!

Look, then, for the practical message and its practical application, remembering that a dream may well have a double message, one to be taken literally, and one to be listened to symbolically as well. Linking the story or series of events together and seen as a play, much will be revealed. Dialogue, puns and word play will come to life and, with the help of a dream dictionary, the more traditional meanings of signs and symbols will be found. Previous associations having been accounted for and the underlying theme discovered, the message should now be recognized. Once having done this, all that remains is to apply this to our own personal situation or circumstances, which we alone know.

DREAM THEMES AND THE ROYAL ROAD

'The interpretations of dreams is the royal road to a knowledge of the subconscious activities of the mind,' said Freud. Using royalty as a dream theme is far more common than most would care to admit. Illusions of grandeur and thinking one is better than the neighbours apart, the royalty theme symbolizes those archetypal forces we were force-fed on as children. Cinderella, Sleeping Beauty, frogs into princes and kings and queens from endless fairy stories, who always end up living happily ever afterwards, are deeply imbedded into our collective unconscious, and whether we are royalists or not, a queen symbolizes the ultimate heroine. She is Venus, the High Priestess, the Queen of Heaven and Mother Earth. She is the personification of the feminine aspect of life itself.

Just as some signs and symbols are used more frequently than others in dreams, so too are certain themes, royalty being just one of them. We all have these basic-theme dreams from time to time, and although in content they are much the same, the messages they convey to the individual dreamer are always different.

THE MANSION OF THE SOUL

The most common of these themes is that of a house or building which we nocturnally inhabit. When we are not dreaming literally this symbolizes the Mansion of the Soul. Each dream house is as different as the dreamer who creates it, and represents him or her as a person. The house is the physical counterpart and the occupier is the dreamer's soul or spirit who flits hauntingly through strange yet half-familiar rooms, ascends and descends staircases, glides along corridors and passages, through doors and under archways. Up in the attic are stored high hopes, some forgotten like dusty relics, whereas down in the cellar are creepy-crawlie things that hide in dark corners. The bedroom is for privacy and sex, whereas in the kitchen we have to face the practical facts of life. The permutations are endless, but the underlying theme is always the same, concerning itself with personal relationships within and around that dream mansion.

The condition of the house, inside and out, reveals physical and mental states of the dreamer. If the action takes place in the attic then ideals, hopes, intuition and intellectual matters are under review, but if the scene is set in the cellar then light will have to be shone on the objects hidden away down there. Throughout the house there will be doors of opportunity; some may be locked, in which case it is the key we need. Stairs might be difficult to climb but well worth the effort, and fires in hearths should be kept burning if enthusiasm is to continue. Windows, representing the eyes of the soul, look out on pastures, parks and gardens, symbolizing a personal Garden of Eden – by no means always an idyllic place. It represents the outside world, the dreamer's environment as he alone sees it. For some the flower beds are overgrown and weeds are taking over, but for others an almost too orderly scene of regimentation suggests that even nature has been robbed and restrained! Who and what comes into this garden, either as welcome visitors or as unwanted intruders, is important, for they represent friends and foes, uniquely but accurately disguised.

WATER THEMES

Water as an underlying theme represents states of emotions and feelings. From watching a babbling brook to experiencing near drowning in fearful raging torrents, the depths and dangers from psychological undercurrents found in ourselves, other people and in situations as a whole, are all thus symbolized. The depth, clearness, cloudiness and turbulence of the water reveal aspects of a problem, so if we weather a storm at sea we know we can overcome a trying time, but if still waters run deep and look murky into the bargain then we are being warned of unseen complications, not to mention possible cross currents.

The theme of a great inundation is a dream experienced by many, and there are two possible interpretations of this. One is that it is a collective premonition of a natural disaster similar to the biblical flood, and the other is that it is purely personal, showing the dreamer that his life is on the point of being overpowered by a great wave of emotion.

BIRTH AND DEATH THEMES

To dream of a birth is said to mean a death, and vice versa. Psychic dreamers often receive telepathic impressions from those about to be born into this world and from those about to depart, so they are well prepared for such events. Most dreams concerning babies, however, symbolize personal potential and hopes for the future for the dream-baby is the brainchild of the dreamer. Symbolically, this tells the dreamer that he has within all that is needed to achieve a lifelong ambition. The theme is the same, but the ambition is different.

Death as a dream theme, on the other hand, always leaves a worrying feeling behind. Although this is mainly a fear that the dream will turn out to be prophetic, as indeed it might, it is primarily a warning at the time of the dream.

Without scenes in our head there is nothing. Imagery, therefore, is the primary way of thinking and being, not primitive, and it is imagery, some literal and some symbolic, that forms our dreams.

NUDITY THEMES

To wander down the road in a vest that is far too short, or even completely in the nude, may seem funny the next day, but it was no joke when it happened most realistically in the dream. The nudity theme was once thought to indicate guilt feelings of a sexual nature, but we now know that these scantily dressed experiences show that the dreamer fears another sort of exposure in public. He feels vulnerable and for all to be revealed would indeed be a disgrace. Clothes represent our outer façade, they are our different characteristics and our personality that usually protects and hides the real us inside. Remove these clothes and it is not the body, but the secret that is bared.

On a more practical level, nudity can simply be a warning that we are revealing too much of ourselves and giving away too many personal secrets.

JOURNEY THEMES

The travelling theme is important, although it often forms part of a much fuller dream. Whether this journey is made by train, boat, car, aeroplane, bike or on foot, it represents our destiny, our way through life. Railway stations, bus stops, airport terminals and petrol stations are all places where we halt and wait to decide in which direction we shall travel next. To miss a bus means we must not panic and although one opportunity has been missed, another, like the next bus, will soon come along. 'Be patient' is the message and remain confident in the future.

HELP AND HEALING THEMES

Help and healing in dreams takes many forms. Nightmares, for example, generally considered to be bad dreams, can be healing processes in themselves. Those associated with illness and fevers which produce a rapid increase of the body's metabolism, making us sweat and our hearts beat madly, sending what seems like a surge of enormous energy through the system, have amazing curative powers. After all, the key to all healing is energy.

PROGRESSION OF DREAMS

The long-term effect from a dream can be everlasting. If a particular dream impresses us, especially if there is a person in it whom we cannot identify as an aspect of ourselves or recognize as someone we know, then we can return to that dream situation when awake and not only have an action-replay but make that person reveal his identity. We created him in our dream so part of us, our dreaming mind, must know who or what that figure represents. To discover this we have to visualize the scene and re-enact it, consciously. When the unidentified figure comes into view we challenge him firmly and so discover whom or what he represents.

It is important, however, to remember that this figure may not be representing a person at all but a figment of our imagination brought in to convey a particular fear or problem. This, symbolized as a person, is exactly what we would expect the dreaming mind to do! Tradition uses a slightly bent-cloaked figure as the advance guard of death, so here is one model for a start. We talk constantly of pathetic figures, angry people and miserable creatures to describe what we think are emotional and psychological states in others, so why should these not enter our dreams exactly as we star them? The answer is that they do! Interpret the trait and we discover the person or state it symbolizes.

DREAMS AND LIFE

Dreams are about life and life is about dreams. It does not seem to matter how many mistakes we make – at our own expense, of course, not other people's – so long as we learn from them. After all, if we knew certain things at the time we would not have done them, thus proving we needed the experience in the first place. Dreams, the greatest gift from ourselves to ourselves, will give us a short-cut to that experience but only if we acknowledge them as sources of great power and enlightenment. We also have to accept that they are, in principle, the same for everyone. We all have prophetic dreams, warning dreams, fear dreams, sexy dreams, psychic dreams and a thousand and one other types of dreams varying in proportion and degree, depending on our way of life and our need of them. If we are content with our lot and do not ask profound cosmic questions then we will not receive profound dreams. There would be no point in them so our dreaming mind does not bother to even hint at such things. On the other hand, if we earnestly seek solutions to creative, unique work, then we will receive from our dreams those original solutions which we seek.

Understanding your dreams helps you to understand not only yourself, but others as well.